# God the Devil and the Internet

---

*"The Online Advantage: Using God's Blueprint to Thrive in a Connected World" Maximize the Internet's Potential for Blessings While Guarding Against Risks."*

---

**Bradley Hawkins**

# Contents

# Part 1

# Creation and Innovation Under God's Sovereignty, Insights into His Masterplan

# Introduction

## The Battle for Your Digital Soul

I remember the first time I realized we were in a war. It wasn't a war fought with bullets or bombs—it was far more subtle and far more dangerous. It was a war for our souls, and the battleground was in a place most of us never expected: the digital world.

I was sitting at my desk in the office of my investment firm, flipping through reports, when a sudden alert popped up on my computer screen. At first, it seemed like a minor glitch, a typical computer issue that could be fixed with a few clicks. But within minutes, I realized that something far more sinister was happening. My system was under attack—files were being locked, my data was being compromised, and everything I had worked so hard to build was at risk.

That moment opened my eyes to the reality we face today: the enemy has found a new way to infiltrate our lives. It's not just through temptation or sin, but through the very technology we use every day. Our smartphones, computers, social media accounts, emails, and cloud-based services have become the front lines of a spiritual battle we can't afford to ignore.

Let me be clear—this book isn't just about technology. It's about **how the enemy is using technology to infiltrate your life, your family, your business, and your spiritual walk with God**. It's about how God, in His infinite wisdom, has also provided **tools, strategies, and divine protection** to help you thrive in the digital age. And it's about how **you can take back control** of your digital life and walk in the abundant life God promises, without falling prey to the enemy's tactics.

# The Digital Battlefield You Didn't See Coming

When we think of spiritual warfare, we often think of temptation, fear, and the age-old struggles between good and evil. We picture the battles that rage in our hearts and minds. But there's another battlefield that many Christians overlook—a battlefield that has become more dangerous and deceptive with every passing year.

Think about it: in the last few decades, the world has changed at a pace we've never seen before. The rise of the internet, artificial intelligence, social media, and cloud computing has transformed how we live, how we work, and how we connect. Technology has the power to bring **tremendous blessings**—it's a gift from God that allows us to reach more people, share the gospel, and expand our impact. But just as every gift from God can be twisted, the enemy has found ways to corrupt this gift, turning it into a tool for **fear, deception, isolation, and destruction**.

The truth is, every time you log on to your computer, every time you swipe through your phone, every time you open an email or download an app—you're stepping onto a digital battlefield. And make no mistake, the stakes are high. If you're not careful, the enemy will use technology to distract you, discourage you, and even destroy the good work God is doing in your life.

You may be thinking, "But I don't understand all this technology. It's too complicated for me." Or maybe you feel overwhelmed by the constant changes in the digital world. Believe me, I get it. I didn't grow up with computers, smartphones, or AI. I've had to **learn and adapt** just like you. But here's the thing—whether you like it or not, we can't avoid the world we live in. **God doesn't want us to run from technology; He wants us to take dominion over it.** He wants us to use the tools He's given us for His glory, not retreat in fear because the enemy has tried to hijack them.

# What's At Stake? Your Soul, Your Family, Your Future

So, what's really at stake in this battle? It's not just your personal data or your online privacy (although those are important). What's at stake is your **spiritual life**, your **family's safety**, your **business's success**, and the **future God has planned for you**. Every day, the enemy is working to undermine your faith, distract your focus, and weaken your ability to walk in God's blessings—all through the subtle power of technology.

Maybe you've already felt the effects. You've noticed how the internet has become a breeding ground for fear and anxiety, how social media creates division and envy, and how digital distractions pull you away from spending time with God and your loved ones. Or maybe you've experienced a cyberattack or a data breach that left you feeling violated and exposed. More specifically, you have noticed that social media algorithms push polarizing content that divides Christian communities. Addictive app designs steal hours of time that could be spent in prayer or with family. Data breaches expose private information that can be used to target believers. Online scams specifically prey on Christian organizations and churches. Perhaps you've sensed that something isn't quite right, that the digital world is offering convenience at the cost of your peace.

Let me tell you, you're not imagining things. **The enemy is using technology to try to pull you away from God's purpose.** But here's the good news: **God has a plan for you, even in the digital age**. And this book is going to show you exactly how to fight back—**spiritually and practically**.

## Why This Book Will Change Your Life

You're holding in your hands a **battle plan**. This book is not just a collection of thoughts and advice—it's a **strategic guide** to reclaiming your life in the digital world. Inside these pages, you're going to learn:

- **How to discern the enemy's tactics** in the digital age: The Bible warns us in 1 Peter 5:8 that "your adversary the devil prowls around like a roaring lion, seeking someone to devour." This is truer now than ever before. The enemy is prowling through cyberspace, looking for ways to steal your time, your attention, and your faith. But this book will give you the tools to see through his schemes and stand strong.
- **How to protect your family and your business from digital attacks:** Proverbs 4:23 tells us to "guard your heart, for everything you do flows from it." In the same way, we must guard our digital lives. You'll learn practical cybersecurity strategies that protect your online presence and safeguard the blessings God has entrusted to you—whether that's your family's safety or your business's success.
- **How to reclaim technology for God's glory:** Ephesians 6:10-18 urges us to put on the "full armor of God" so we can stand against the enemy's attacks. This book will show you how to use spiritual and practical tools to take control of the digital world and **use it to advance God's kingdom**. You'll learn how to turn what the enemy meant for harm into a powerful weapon for good.
- **How to walk in abundance** in the digital age: Jesus said in John 10:10, "The thief comes only to steal and kill and destroy; I have come that they may have life and have it to the full." Technology doesn't have to be a source of fear or distraction—it can be a source of **abundance**. Through the principles in this book, you'll learn how to embrace the gifts God has given you, including technology, and use them to live a **full, abundant life**.

This book is going to change the way you see the world. It's going to give you new eyes to see **how God is working** through technology and **how the enemy is trying to stop you**. But more importantly, it's going to give you the **confidence, wisdom, and spiritual tools** you need to take back control and walk in the abundant life God has promised you.

So, are you ready? Are you ready to step into this battle and claim victory? Are you ready to use technology for good, to protect your family, and to advance God's kingdom? If so, then let's begin. Together, we're going to fight for what matters most, and we're going to win—not because we're strong, but because **God is with us**.

Let's take back the digital world for God's glory. It's time to fight, to reclaim, and to walk in the fullness of His promises.

Welcome to God, the Devil, and the Internet. Let's get started.

# Chapter 1

## God Creates It All

### God as the Source of All Creation and Innovation

In today's world, it's easy to credit human achievement to personal effort, education, and innovation, especially in fields like technology. We often hear phrases like "self-made," "I figured it out," or "I was trained for this," but there is a foundational truth that needs to be understood: **God is the Creator of all.** He is the one who gives us the ability, strength, and wisdom to create. This includes not only those who openly acknowledge Him but even those who may not believe or give glory to God for their talents.

### God as the Source of Strength and Wisdom

The Bible consistently reminds us that **God is the ultimate source of all wisdom, knowledge, and ability.** In the book of **Exodus**, God gives specific people the wisdom and skills to create the sacred objects for the tabernacle:

*"Then the Lord said to Moses, 'See, I have chosen Bezalel son of Uri, the son of Hur, of the tribe of Judah, and I have filled him with the Spirit of God, with wisdom, with understanding, with knowledge and with all kinds of skills—to make artistic designs for work in gold, silver, and bronze, to cut and set stones, to work in wood, and to engage in all kinds of crafts.'" (Exodus 31:1-5)*

This passage shows us that God is directly involved in giving people the talent and skill to innovate and create. Just as He gave Bezalel the ability to craft beautiful things for His glory, God continues to give us wisdom, understanding, and creativity. Whether we use those talents to build technology, design structures, or invent new things, it is ultimately God who empowers us to do so.

## The Natural "Bent" Given by God

Each of us has a unique "bent"—a natural inclination or talent that sets us apart. This bent is God-given. Whether someone is a gifted engineer, an artist, or a brilliant thinker, those talents are given by the Creator. We see this truth reflected in **James 1:17**:

*"Every good and perfect gift is from above, coming down from the Father of the heavenly lights, who does not change like shifting shadows." (James 1:17)*

We often attribute our achievements to hard work, education, or natural ability, but even these attributes are gifts from God. He is the One who gives us life and the ability to think, innovate, and create. It is **His breath** that fills our lungs, and **His Spirit** that guides our steps

## Human Achievements: God's Work Through Us

Even when people do not acknowledge God, He remains the source of their abilities. A person may claim their knowledge is self-earned through education or personal discovery, but **God is the One who provides the very ability to learn, reason, and create**.

Consider this verse from **Deuteronomy 8:18**:

*"But remember the Lord your God, for it is He who gives you the ability to produce wealth, and so confirms His covenant, which He swore to your ancestors, as it is today." (Deuteronomy 8:18)*

This reminds us that even our capacity to generate wealth, create new technologies, or discover new ideas is granted by God. No matter how much someone might claim to be "self-made," God is still the One who gave them the ability, the resources, and the opportunity to achieve anything.

# Technology as a Gift from God

We live in a time of unprecedented technological advancement, and while it's tempting to credit human ingenuity alone, the Bible teaches us that **all wisdom comes from God**. Just as God gave Solomon incredible wisdom to govern Israel (1 Kings 4:29-34), He also gives modern inventors and technologists the knowledge to develop the innovations we use today.

Consider **Colossians 1:16**, which tells us that everything is created through God:

*"For in Him all things were created: things in heaven and on earth, visible and invisible, whether thrones or powers or rulers or authorities; all things have been created through Him and for Him."* *(Colossians 1:16)*

God created everything we see today, from the simplest app to the most complex AI system. His creative power flows through every innovation and breakthrough.Even artificial intelligence, one of today's most advanced technologies. While engineers write the code, the very principles that make AI possible, pattern recognition, learning from experience, problem-solving, are all based on systems God already created in the human brain. Even when people do not give credit to God, He remains the Creator of all things, visible and invisible. The phone in your hand, the computer on your desk, the medical breakthroughs that save lives—all these exist because God gave humanity the knowledge and skill to create them.

## Why We Look to God as the Creator

God, in His infinite wisdom, created not just the natural world but also endowed us with the intellectual capacity to innovate within it. **Genesis 1:27** tells us that we are made in God's image:

*"So God created mankind in His own image, in the image of God He created them; male and female He created them."* *(Genesis 1:27)*

Being created in God's image means that we reflect His creativity, wisdom, and ability to bring things into existence. Just as God created the heavens and the earth, He has given us the ability to use our minds to create and develop the world around us.

However, it is important to remember that all our achievements are only possible because of **God's sustaining power. Hebrews 1:3** says:

*"The Son is the radiance of God's glory and the exact representation of His being, sustaining all things by His powerful word."* (Hebrews 1:3)

This verse reminds us that it is by God's word that all things are sustained. Without Him, nothing could continue to exist, let alone thrive or grow.

This understanding of God as the ultimate Creator should transform how we approach technology development and innovation. Instead of asking "What can I create?", we begin asking "What has God enabled me to discover and develop?" This shift in perspective changes everything—from how we approach problems to how we handle success.

## The Humility of True Understanding

When we begin to understand that all we have—our knowledge, skills, creativity, and opportunities—come from God, it humbles us. **1 Corinthians 4:7** asks:

*"For who makes you different from anyone else? What do you have that you did not receive? And if you did receive it, why do you boast as though you did not?"* (1 Corinthians 4:7)

This passage encourages us to recognize that **all things are gifts from God**, and we should live in a posture of humility and gratitude rather than boasting about our own achievements. The moment we understand that **we can do nothing apart from God**, we start to live with a deeper sense of purpose and dependence on Him.

14

# Conclusion: Our Role as Stewards of God-Given Talent

At the end of the day, all human achievement points back to God, whether people recognize it or not. **God is the source of all knowledge, wisdom, and skill**, and He deserves the glory for every good and perfect gift. Whether it's the latest technological breakthrough or a simple act of kindness, it all flows from the Creator.

Let us give glory to God, remembering the words of **Proverbs 3:6**:

*"In all your ways acknowledge Him, and He will make your paths straight."* (Proverbs 3:6)

When we acknowledge God as the source of all we have, He directs our paths, and we walk in His purpose, using the talents and skills He gave us for His glory.

## Reflection and Action:

- Reflect on the talents God has given you.
- Acknowledge that these gifts are from God, not self-made.
- Use your abilities to bring glory to Him, recognizing that without Him, you can do nothing.
- Encourage others to see the Creator behind their abilities, helping them recognize that God is the ultimate source of all.

# Chapter 2

## God's Creation the Industrial Revolution

As we explored in the previous chapter, God is the source of all creation and innovation. From my perspective, the **internet and computer systems** are among the greatest inventions of all time, possibly rivaled only by the **Industrial Revolution**. Both of these technological advancements have transformed the way we live, work, and connect, and I believe they are **gifts from God**, created through the minds of people He is blessed with wisdom and creativity. **James 1:17** tells us that *"Every good and perfect gift is from above,"* and these inventions are no exception. The internet and computers have allowed for incredible advancements in communication, healthcare, education, and business, expanding human potential in ways we couldn't have imagined. When we explore these great inventions, we can see how **God's faithfulness** continues to work through people, giving them the knowledge and tools to create systems that reflect His desire for **connection, productivity, and progress**. Even in a world where these gifts can be misused, God's hand in their creation shines through, showing His ongoing commitment to providing for His people and fulfilling His promises.

## God's Hand in the Industrial Revolution, the Internet, and Modern Technology: A History of His Providence

Throughout human history, God has been at work, even when we may not fully recognize His influence or give Him the credit He deserves. The advancements of the Industrial Revolution and the subsequent development of the Internet are no exception. These monumental shifts in society and technology were not just the result of human ingenuity; they were part of God's grand design to equip humanity for the work of His Kingdom, providing for His children and enabling the spread of the Gospel.

The Bible reminds us that **God is sovereign over all human activity** and accomplishments. In **Proverbs 16:9**, it says,

*"In their hearts humans plan their course, but the Lord establishes their steps."*

This verse points to the reality that while humanity may think they are the creators and drivers of history, it is **God who directs every development**, every invention, and every revolution for His greater purpose.

## God's Wisdom in Historical Developments

*Isaiah 55:9 says, "As the heavens are higher than the earth, so are my ways higher than your ways and my thoughts than your thoughts."*

We may not always see or understand how God works through human history, but the Bible assures us that **His ways are beyond our comprehension** and that He is always working for our good (Romans 8:28). The Industrial Revolution and the rise of the Internet, two of the most profound and influential overarching inventions that God created through men, are prime examples of how God's wisdom and knowledge have permeated human progress, even when humanity has not always recognized or glorified Him for it.

# The Industrial Revolution: The Foundation of Modern Society

## A Deeper Dive into the Origins

The Industrial Revolution, which began in the late 18th century and continued into the 19th, was **a divinely orchestrated moment in human history** that revolutionized economies and societies around the world. Prior to this period, most economies were agrarian, meaning people relied on farming and manual labor to survive. Life was difficult, and the vast majority of people lived in poverty. However, **God saw the growing needs of humanity**—a world population that was rapidly expanding and needed new ways of producing goods, food, and wealth.

The birth of the Industrial Revolution occurred largely in **Great Britain**, a country that was uniquely positioned for such a transformation. The combination of **scientific advancements**, **available capital**, **natural resources**, and **political stability** created the perfect conditions for industrial growth. However, these developments were not purely coincidental. **God was orchestrating these circumstances**, providing the environment needed for such a significant change to take place.

## Key Inventions and Their Spiritual Implications

The Industrial Revolution brought forth machines that transformed entire industries. These groundbreaking inventions enhanced productivity in ways that previous generations could barely imagine. Each innovation demonstrated God's wisdom working through human creativity. These included:

- **The spinning jenny** (1764), created by **James Hargreaves**, which allowed for the mass production of yarn.

- **The steam engine**, developed by **James Watt** (1765), revolutionized transportation and industry, allowing factories to operate with greater efficiency.
- **The power loom** (1785), invented by **Edmund Cartwright**, which mechanized weaving and further advanced the textile industry.
- **The cotton gin** (1793), invented by **Eli Whitney**, which transformed the cotton industry by making it easier to separate cotton fibers from seeds.

Each of these inventions played a crucial role in shaping the modern economy. However, behind each invention was **God's hand guiding the minds of the inventors**, granting them the wisdom and knowledge to create tools that would bless humanity.

The Bible speaks about this kind of divine wisdom in **Exodus 35:30-35**, where God equips artisans with the skills to build the tabernacle:

"Then Moses said to the Israelites, 'See, the Lord has chosen Bezalel... and he has filled him with the Spirit of God, with wisdom, with understanding, with knowledge and with all kinds of skills.'"

Just as God gave Bezalel the skill to create beautiful works for His glory, He also gave inventors and innovators during the Industrial Revolution the wisdom and ability to build machines that would improve the quality of life for millions.

## The Benefits of the Industrial Revolution: God's Provision for His People

### Economic Growth and Social Progress

The Industrial Revolution was **not without its challenges**—factories were often dangerous places to work, and child labor was a significant issue. But over time, **God used this period of history to bring about greater prosperity**, allowing for economic growth and social progress that lifted millions out of poverty. By increasing the productivity of goods, the Industrial Revolution made items like clothing, food, and tools more affordable and accessible to more people.

Industries such as steel production, transportation (with the advent of the steam locomotive), and manufacturing grew rapidly, allowing cities to expand and new opportunities to arise. People who once had limited opportunities in agrarian societies now had jobs in factories, mills, and railroads. Though many faced hardships, **God used these advancements to provide for His children**, ensuring that people could support their families and communities.

## Exploitation and Inequality: The Dark Side of the Industrial Revolution

During the Industrial Revolution, some individuals and corporations exploited the rapid economic growth to amass wealth at the expense of workers and society. Greedy factory owners prioritized profit over human dignity, forcing laborers, including children, to work long hours in unsafe, grueling conditions for meager wages. These exploitative practices led to widespread poverty, poor health, and harsh living conditions for workers, who often lived in overcrowded slums with little access to basic necessities. This unchecked exploitation fueled social inequality, deepened class divisions, and triggered labor unrest, as workers were treated as disposable tools rather than human beings deserving of rights and fair treatment. The lack of regulations allowed these abuses to flourish, creating lasting damage to society by fostering systemic poverty and exploitation.

## Social Reforms and God's Justice

Despite the difficulties of early industrial life, **God continued to work through social reformers** like **William Wilberforce** and **Robert Owen**, who fought for workers' rights, improved conditions, and ended child labor. Their work was a reflection of God's justice, as seen in **Proverbs 31:8-9**:

*"Speak up for those who cannot speak for themselves, for the rights of all who are destitute. Speak up and judge fairly; defend the rights of the poor and needy."*

Their efforts improved the lives of millions, and they believed in a **God-ordained purpose to care for the weak and oppressed**.

# Story Time: God's Provision with the Industrial Revolution

## A Story of God's Provision: The Industrial Revolution and the Lives It Transformed

Occasionally in this book, I will break the flow and style to include a story that illustrates the point I'm making. Let's let John's journey explain this one.

In the quiet town of **Lancashire**, England, the year was **1774**, and the world was on the cusp of something extraordinary. The dawn of the Industrial Revolution had arrived, though no one quite realized it yet. The soft clinking of looms and spinning wheels filled the air, as farmers and weavers went about their daily work—most unaware that their entire way of life was about to change. They had prayed for provision, for more food on the table, for better opportunities, and for relief from the exhausting work that barely kept them afloat. What they didn't know was that **God was already working** behind the scenes, preparing to bless them in ways they couldn't even imagine.

**John's Journey: A Weaver's Dream**, a humble weaver in Lancashire, spent his days working tirelessly to produce cloth by hand, a painstaking process that required endless hours of labor. His family often went without proper food, despite his relentless efforts. But John trusted in **God's provision**, praying daily for an answer to his family's needs.

*"The Lord is my shepherd; I shall not want."* (Psalm 23:1) These words of David echoed in John's heart, though he couldn't see how God would provide.

Then one day, John heard whispers of a **new invention** called the **spinning jenny**. It was said to make the production of yarn much faster, increasing efficiency tenfold. At first, it sounded too good to be true. Could it really change his life? He prayed again, asking God for wisdom. When a friend invited him to see the machine in action, John stood in awe. The spinning jenny, designed by **James Hargreaves**, was operating before his eyes, spinning multiple threads at once with ease.

Tears welled up in John's eyes as he saw it for what it was—**God's answer to his prayers**. He understood that God had given Hargreaves the wisdom to create this machine, and it was a blessing for people like him. He knew he needed to walk in obedience to this new opportunity, trusting that God was leading him.

John sold his handloom and invested in a spinning jenny. His productivity increased, and soon he was able to provide for his family in ways he never thought possible. **God was his provider**, and through this new invention, John's life was transformed. He no longer worked from dawn to dusk for mere survival; now, he saw the fruit of his labor multiply, just as God had promised.

*"And God is able to bless you abundantly, so that in all things at all times, having all that you need, you will abound in every good work."* (2 Corinthians 9:8)

**Sarah's New Beginning: From Poverty to Prosperity** Meanwhile, in the city of **Manchester**, **Sarah**, a widow, struggled to feed her two children. She worked as a seamstress, but the income barely covered their basic needs. Every night, she knelt in prayer, asking God for a breakthrough. *"Lord, you promised to take care of the widows and the fatherless. Please, I need Your provision,"* she whispered into the silence.

Then came the news that **factories** were opening across Manchester. Sarah's neighbors spoke of new machines—**power looms, steam engines**, and **mills**—that were capable of producing more goods than ever before. The economy was changing, and the industrialist's needed workers.

Sarah was terrified. She knew nothing of machines, only how to sew by hand. But God had promised to take care of her. She thought of the story of the widow in **1 Kings 17:14-16**, where Elijah told the widow of Zarephath that her jar of flour would not be used up, nor her jug of oil run dry because the Lord would provide during the famine.

*"For this is what the Lord, the God of Israel, says: 'The jar of flour will not be used up and the jug of oil will not run dry until the day the Lord sends rain on the land.'"*

Trusting in that same God, Sarah went to a nearby factory and asked for work. She was hired to operate one of the new machines, and what she experienced amazed her. The machine allowed her to work more efficiently than ever before, and soon her wages increased. She was able to feed her children, clothe them in better garments, and even save for the future. God had not only answered her prayers but **blessed her with more than she had hoped for**.

Sarah's story was just one among many. Thousands of women and men across England began to experience the blessing of **God's provision** through the technological advancements of the Industrial Revolution. Factories rose across the landscape, and with them came jobs, prosperity, and the ability to break free from the chains of poverty. God was showing His children that even in the midst of societal upheaval, **He was their Provider**.

## The Larger Picture: God's Provision for Nations as
John and Sarah's lives changed, so did the economies around them. What once had been small, rural economies dependent on handcrafting became **thriving industrial powerhouses**. The revolution spread from England to Europe, then across the Atlantic to America. Nations

began to trade more efficiently, moving goods at speeds that would have been unimaginable just a few years earlier.

Cities expanded, industries flourished, and **God's provision** reached not only individuals but entire communities. Where once there was hunger, now there was abundance. Where once people toiled endlessly for little reward, now they saw the fruit of their labor multiply. This was more than a shift in technology; this was **God's divine provision at work**.

**Matthew's Obedience: From Field to Factory Matthew**, a farmer in the English countryside, had watched his crops fail year after year. He was tired, weary, and ready to give up. One day, while reading his Bible, he came across **Genesis 1:28**:

*"God blessed them and said to them, 'Be fruitful and increase in number; fill the earth and subdue it. Rule over the fish in the sea and the birds in the sky and over every living creature that moves on the ground.'"*

Matthew knew that God had given humanity the authority to innovate and create. He had heard about the **steam engine**, a powerful new invention that was changing the way people worked. The idea of leaving his family farm and going to work in a factory was daunting, but he felt God was calling him to trust and obey.

Following God's leading, Matthew sold his land and moved to the city to work in a **textile mill** powered by the steam engine. At first, it was difficult to adjust to the new way of life. The machines were loud, and the work was demanding, but over time, Matthew saw God's blessings unfold. His income increased, and he began to save enough money to send his children to school—something he had never thought possible. He realized that the **steam engine wasn't just a machine**; it was a gift from God, created to **ease the burden of work** and to help people live better, more prosperous lives.

*"For I know the plans I have for you," declares the Lord, "plans to prosper you and not to harm you, plans to give you hope and a future."* (Jeremiah 29:11)

# God's Greater Purpose: Why the Industrial Revolution?

But why did God allow such a massive shift to take place? Why did He bless individuals with the wisdom to create machines like the spinning jenny, the steam engine, and the power loom? The answer lies in God's heart as a **Provider**. He promised to care for His children, and as the world grew, the needs of His children increased. The **Industrial Revolution** was one of the ways God ensured that the growing population would have enough food, clothing, and shelter.

- **Job 12:13**:"To God belong wisdom and power; counsel and understanding are His."

  God used His infinite wisdom to inspire the minds of inventors and innovators. They may have thought they were creating for their own purposes, but in reality, **God was using them as instruments** to bless His people.

- **Philippians 4:19**:"And my God will meet all your needs according to the riches of His glory in Christ Jesus."

  Through the advancements of the Industrial Revolution, God was meeting the needs of millions of people. He provided them with jobs, income, and the ability to care for their families.

# The Emotional Impact: Experiencing God's Abundance

For the average person, the Industrial Revolution was **both exhilarating and overwhelming**. On the one hand, it brought about new opportunities, better jobs, and the ability to provide for their families in ways they had never experienced before. On the other hand, the rapid pace of change was unsettling. People had to adapt to new ways of working and living, and many struggled with the transition.

But for those who trusted in **God's provision**, the revolution was a profound answer to prayer. **God's blessings** flowed through the machines, the factories, and the new economic systems, just as much as they flowed through the crops in the field or the work of a fisherman's hands. God had not abandoned His people; rather, He had **equipped them for the future**.

Conclusion: Walking in Obedience and Trust

The stories of John, Sarah, and Matthew represent countless individuals whose lives were transformed by the Industrial Revolution. God, in His wisdom and love, blessed humanity with the inventions that made life easier, more productive, and more prosperous. Whether they were weavers, factory workers, or farmers, God provided for them as He promised.

*"Look at the birds of the air; they do not sow or reap or store away in barns, and yet your heavenly Father feeds them. Are you not much more valuable than them?"* (Matthew 6:26)

Through the steam engines, the factories, and the spinning jennies, God took care of His children. And just as He provided then, He continues to provide today. Whether through the development of new technologies or the rise of new industries, God's hand is always at work, ensuring that His beloved children have everything they need.

## God's Covenant and the Industrial Revolution: A Gift of Choice and Consequence

The **Industrial Revolution**, one of the most significant shifts in human history, was not just a technological breakthrough but also a

**fulfillment of God's covenantal promises**. God blessed humanity with the ingenuity and creativity necessary to revolutionize industries, economies, and societies. However, as with all of God's gifts, the Industrial Revolution presented **a choice**: to use these gifts for **good** or **evil**. **Free will**—a gift given by God since the beginning of creation—allows us to decide how we will use the blessings He provides. Some choose to **honor God** with their resources and opportunities, while others may choose to misuse them for personal gain, exploitation, or harm. Yet, throughout it all, **God remains sovereign**, continuing to work for the good of those who love Him and seeking to redeem even those who stray.

## God's Covenants: A History of Blessings and Free Will

God's covenants are foundational to understanding His relationship with humanity. Beginning with the **Abrahamic Covenant** (Genesis 12:2-3), God promised to **bless** Abraham and make his descendants a **great nation**. These blessings were not only spiritual but also material, as God promised to provide land, prosperity, and protection. Later, the **Mosaic Covenant** expanded on these promises, giving God's people a law to guide them in how to live righteous lives. **Deuteronomy 28** outlines both the **blessings** of obedience—prosperity, safety, and abundance—and the **curses** of disobedience, including poverty, oppression, and destruction.

God's **Davidic Covenant** promised an eternal kingdom through David's lineage, fulfilled in Jesus Christ, who brings the ultimate blessing to both Jews and Gentiles. Through the **New Covenant** (Jeremiah 31:31-34), established through Jesus' sacrifice, the promises of **provision**, **blessing**, and **relationship** with God were extended to **all believers**, whether Jew or Gentile. **Romans 10:12** makes it clear:

*"For there is no difference between Jew and Gentile—the same Lord is Lord of all and richly blesses all who call on Him."*

With these covenants came **responsibility**. God provided His people with **gifts**, but they had the choice to **obey** or **disobey**. Free will was evident throughout the Bible, starting from the Garden of Eden, where Adam and Eve chose to disobey God, leading to their expulsion and the introduction of sin into the world. Even though **God redeems** through Jesus, the reality of **choice** and **consequences** remains.

## The Industrial Revolution: A Gift That Could Be Used for Good or Bad

The **Industrial Revolution** is a perfect example of a **gift from God** that could be used for **good** or **bad**, depending on the choices of individuals. As God blessed humanity with new technologies—such as the **spinning jenny**, **steam engines**, and **power looms**—people were given the opportunity to use these tools to **bless others**, improve living conditions, and honor God. **Proverbs 8:12** says, *"I, wisdom, dwell with prudence, and I find knowledge and discretion."* God's wisdom was clearly at work, providing the knowledge and discretion to innovate and improve the world.

For example, many used the Industrial Revolution to provide **fair wages**, improve **productivity**, and create **economic growth** that benefited entire communities. Factories provided jobs, towns grew, and more people had access to goods that were once out of reach. Those who sought to honor God in their work, like **William Hayes** in the earlier story, recognized that their success was a gift from God and sought to **use it for good**. They treated their workers fairly, used their resources to bless others, and glorified God with their success. **Proverbs 16:3** reminds us, *"Commit to the Lord whatever you do, and He will establish your plans."*

However, **free will** meant that not everyone chose to use these blessings for good. Others, like **Edward Collins**, used the

Industrial Revolution to **exploit** their workers, grow their wealth at the expense of others, and become consumed by greed. They ignored God's call to **justice and righteousness**, choosing instead to prioritize profits over people. **1 Timothy 6:10** warns us, *"For the love of money is a root of all kinds of evil. Some people, eager for money, have wandered from the faith and pierced themselves with many griefs."* The consequences of this misuse were severe—**poor working conditions, inequality,** and **social unrest**.

Yet even in this darkness, **God continued to work**. He never gives up on His people, even when they misuse His gifts. He continually calls out to those who have strayed, offering them a chance to turn back to Him. **Romans 2:4** tells us that *"God's kindness is intended to lead you to repentance."* He pursues those who choose to use their blessings wrongly, trying to bring them back into alignment with His purposes.

## God's Redemption and Sovereignty: Working for Good Even in the Bad

Even when people use His gifts for **evil**, God has the power to **redeem**. **Romans 8:28** reminds us, *"And we know that in all things God works for the good of those who love Him, who have been called according to His purpose."* Even in the darkest moments of exploitation and greed during the Industrial Revolution, God was working to **redeem** the situation. Social reformers like **William Wilberforce** and **Robert Owen** fought for better working conditions, the abolition of child labor, and fair wages. These efforts were examples of **God's justice** being enacted on earth, as He worked through those who sought to align with His will.

But **free will** remains. God offers redemption, but individuals must choose to **accept it**. Those who continued to walk in disobedience and exploitation still faced the consequences for their choices. **Galatians**

**6:7** warns, *"Do not be deceived: God cannot be mocked. A man reaps what he sows."* Those who sowed **injustice** and **greed** reaped the consequences—whether in the form of societal backlash, business collapse, or personal emptiness. God's desire is always for people to turn back to Him, but He also allows people to experience the **consequences of their actions** when they choose not to listen.

In contrast, those who sought to honor God during the Industrial Revolution experienced **blessing** upon blessing. **Psalm 1:3** says, *"That person is like a tree planted by streams of water, which yields its fruit in season and whose leaf does not wither—whatever they do prospers."* For those who used the gifts of the Industrial Revolution to bless others and honor God, prosperity followed, not just in material wealth but in **relationships**, **community growth**, and **spiritual abundance**. The workers in **God-fearing factories** were treated fairly, experienced improved working conditions, and saw their own families thrive.

## Free Will and Consequences: Choosing Wisely or Suffering the Fallout

The **Industrial Revolution** serves as a stark reminder that **God's gifts can be used for good or for bad**, and the choice lies with each of us. **Free will** is central to God's design. He does not force us to use His blessings in a specific way, but He calls us to choose wisely. **Deuteronomy 30:19** lays it out clearly:

*"This day I call the heavens and the earth as witnesses against you that I have set before your life and death, blessings and curses. Now choose life so that you and your children may live."*

God gives us the **freedom to choose**, but with that freedom comes **responsibility**. Those who choose to use their blessings for **good** will experience the **fruit of righteousness**, as **Isaiah 3:10** says, *"Tell the righteous it will be well with them, for they will enjoy the fruit of their deeds."* However, those who misuse God's gifts for selfish gain, exploitation, or harm will experience the **consequences** of their actions, as **Proverbs 11:18** warns, *"A wicked person earns deceptive wages, but the one who sows righteousness reaps a sure reward."*

Ultimately, **God's heart** is for redemption. He never stops pursuing those who have chosen the wrong path. He continually calls them back to Himself, offering opportunities for repentance and restoration. But even in His grace, **free will** means that not everyone will listen, and there will be consequences for those who persist in **choosing bad** over good. **2 Peter 3:9** reassures us of God's patience, saying, *"The Lord is not slow in keeping His promise, as some understand slowness. Instead, He is patient with you, not wanting anyone to perish, but everyone to come to repentance."*

## Conclusion: God's Gifts, Our Choices, and the Ever-Present Call to Righteousness

The **Industrial Revolution** and the gifts it brought were **tools given by God**, meant to bless and provide for humanity. But, like all of God's gifts, they came with a choice: to use them for good or for bad. **Free will** gives us the opportunity to align our actions with God's purposes or to misuse His blessings for selfish gain. While some used the Industrial Revolution to honor God, treat others fairly, and improve society, others fell into greed, exploitation, and oppression. Yet through it all, **God remains sovereign**, working for the good of those who love Him and continually calling back those who stray.

God's desire is that we would all choose to use His gifts for **good**, aligning ourselves with His **justice, mercy, and love**. When we choose wisely, we experience His **blessings**, and those around us are blessed as well. When we choose poorly, there are consequences, but God never gives up on us. He is always working to **redeem**, to restore, and to bring us back into alignment with His will. **The choice is ours**—to use His gifts for His glory, or to misuse them for selfish gain—but **God will always be there**, inviting us to choose **life**.

God's gifts can be used for good or for evil. God will not eliminate his inventions or gifts if someone uses it for bad. He will keep working on the hearts of people to use his inventions for good.

## Story Time A Tale of Two Industrialists: A Story of Greed, Redemption, and God's Providence

In the bustling city of **Manchester**, where smokestacks rose to the sky and the hum of machinery filled the air, two men began their journeys to success. The **Industrial Revolution** was in full swing, and the opportunities seemed limitless. **William Hayes** and **Edward Collins**, childhood friends turned fierce competitors, both found themselves at the forefront of this new economy, eager to provide for their families and bring prosperity to their community.

God had blessed the world with new technologies—**steam engines**, **power looms**, and **factories**—and people marveled at the speed at which life was changing. What once took hours of backbreaking labor could now be done in a fraction of the time. It was clear to everyone that this revolution was **a gift from God**, a new way for Him to provide for His beloved people. **Isaiah 45:12** echoed the truth that,

*"It is I who made the earth and created mankind on it; my own hands stretched out the heavens; I marshaled their starry hosts."*

Yet, as with any blessing, how one chose to handle it made all the difference.

## The Beginnings: A Shared Vision

Both William and Edward began with **humble intentions**. They saw the potential of the new economy as a way to lift their families out of poverty and to benefit their community. They opened textile factories, employing men, women, and even children from the surrounding villages. There was excitement in the air, the kind of excitement that comes when **God's blessings** seem to be raining down from heaven.

**William Hayes**, a man of quiet faith, often prayed as he expanded his business, asking for wisdom and guidance.

*"Commit to the Lord whatever you do, and He will establish your plans."* (Proverbs 16:3)

Edward, on the other hand, was less inclined to rely on prayer, though he was quick to agree that the Industrial Revolution was a gift from God. He was focused on using this opportunity to get ahead, but he still had good intentions—after all, wasn't providing jobs a good thing?

For the first few years, both men saw **unprecedented success**. Their factories grew, their workers were paid well, and the towns around them flourished. But as their fortunes increased, so did their ambitions. Soon, they weren't just thinking about providing for their families; they were consumed with thoughts of **expansion, competition, and wealth**.

## The Fall into Greed

As their businesses grew, **greed began to take root** in both men. William, once a humble factory owner, started to look at his profits with more desire than gratitude. He expanded his business aggressively, buying up smaller competitors and cutting costs wherever he could, often at the expense of his workers. Edward followed suit, growing his business even faster, though he did so with a ruthlessness that shocked even those close to him.

Both men began competing fiercely. They undercut each other's prices, spread rumors about the other's factories, and engaged in dishonest business practices to gain an advantage. **The Industrial Revolution** brought wealth, but it also exposed the darker sides of human ambition. **1 Timothy 6:10** warns,

*"For the love of money is the root of all kinds of evil. Some people, eager for money, have wandered from the faith and pierced themselves with many griefs."*

The warning was there, but neither William nor Edward seemed to hear it. Workers were laid off when profits weren't high enough. Wages were cut. Conditions in the factories deteriorated as both men focused more on **profits than people**. They had begun with the intention of using **God's blessing** to help their community, but now they were **using people** to gain even more wealth.

## God's Call: The Battle for the Soul

God, in His mercy, tried to get the attention of both men. He sent subtle and not-so-subtle reminders that they were going down a dangerous path.

For William, it began with **small convictions**. He would sit in church on Sunday and hear sermons that seemed to speak directly to his heart. **"Do not store up for yourselves treasures on earth, where moths and vermin destroy, and where thieves break in and steal."** (Matthew 6:19) The words gnawed at him, but he ignored them. There was always business to attend to, and the voice of ambition spoke louder than the voice of God.

For Edward, the signs were even clearer. **Accidents began happening in his factories**—machines malfunctioned, workers got injured, and the local community started to turn against him. Still, he refused to listen. He told himself that these were just the costs of doing business. He could still remember how hard life had been when he had nothing, and he wasn't about to give it all up now.

Yet, **God's voice never ceases**, and He continues to call both men back to Him.

# The Turning Point: A Heart Surrendered

One night, **William** had a dream. In the dream, he was standing in a grand hall filled with gold and silver, treasures beyond imagination. He was reaching out to touch them when suddenly, the floor beneath him gave way. He fell into a deep pit, surrounded by darkness. He heard a voice—**God's voice**—saying, *"You have chosen the wrong treasure."* He woke in a cold sweat, realizing that his pursuit of wealth had blinded him to what truly mattered.

The next morning, William went to his office, stared at the papers showing his massive profits, and knew he needed to change. **He prayed** for the first time in months, asking for God's forgiveness and guidance. He remembered **Matthew 6:33**:

*"But seek first His kingdom and His righteousness, and all these things will be given to you as well."*

From that day forward, William decided to **honor God** with his business. He reinstated fair wages for his workers, improved working conditions, and committed to using his wealth to serve others rather than himself. His employees began to feel the difference immediately. They were no longer overworked and underpaid. Instead, they were treated with respect and dignity, and they prospered under William's new leadership. **God had transformed his heart**, and the blessings flowed out to everyone around him.

# Edward's Downfall: A Life Without God

Meanwhile, **Edward** continued his greedy path. His wealth grew, but so did his discontent. No matter how much money he made, it was never enough. He treated his workers harshly, expecting more and more from them without giving anything in return. He was constantly looking over his shoulder, paranoid that someone would take his fortune away.

While God had tried to get his attention, **Edward's heart remained hardened**. He refused to see the accidents in his factories as warnings. He refused to acknowledge that his business was built on **dishonesty and exploitation**. One day, a fire broke out in one of his largest factories, devastating his operations. Workers were injured, and his reputation was tarnished. Still, Edward blamed others, never taking responsibility for his actions or turning to God.

The Bible speaks of those who pursue wealth at the expense of righteousness:

*"Whoever loves money never has enough; whoever loves wealth is never satisfied with their income. This too is meaningless."* (Ecclesiastes 5:10)

Edward's pursuit of wealth without God had left him empty, and his business began to crumble. His employees, though they continued to work for him, were demoralized, overworked, and struggling to provide for their families. **God still blessed them**, but life was hard under Edward's greed-driven leadership.

## The Impact of Obedience: God's Blessing on William's Factory

In contrast, **William's factory flourished**. As he honored God with his business, God honored him in return. His workers were not just employees—they were part of a community. William started programs to educate the children of his workers, providing schooling that would help them rise above their circumstances. He gave generously to local charities and built homes for those in need. His factory became known as a place of **honesty, integrity, and fairness**.

His workers experienced the truth of **Psalm 37:4**:

*"Take delight in the Lord, and He will give you the desires of your heart."*

36

They were not only paid fair wages but also experienced a sense of purpose and belonging. The atmosphere in William's factory was one of joy, cooperation, and faith. **God's presence** was felt in the daily operations, and it became clear that when a business was run according to **God's principles**, everyone prospered.

## Conclusion: The Path of Blessing or the Path of Greed

In the end, both William and Edward had started with **good intentions**, but only one had chosen to follow God's call. **William's obedience** led to a business that blessed not only him and his family but everyone around him. **Edward's greed**, on the other hand, left him with broken relationships, lost opportunities, and an empty soul.

**God is faithful**, and even when we stray, He continually calls us back to Him. For William, that call was answered, and through his obedience, **God was glorified**. For Edward, the call went unheeded, and while God still blessed his workers, life was harder for those under his leadership.

The story of these two men serves as a reminder that **God's blessings are abundant** when we follow His Word and live according to His principles. Wealth and success may come, but true prosperity—the kind that blesses not only ourselves but also everyone around us—comes only when we seek first the Kingdom of God.

The **Industrial Revolution**, like any great advancement in human history, was neither inherently good nor bad—it was a **tool given by God** for humanity to use. God allows us to create, innovate, and advance in ways that can improve life and glorify Him. But the key lies in **how we choose** to use those tools. **Proverbs 3:5-6** tells us to, *"Trust in the Lord with all your heart and lean not on your own understanding; in all your ways submit to Him, and He will make your paths straight."* The Industrial Revolution provided opportunities for innovation and economic growth, but whether it became a blessing, or a curse depended on the hearts of the people using it. Those who sought to honor God with their businesses and technology could use these tools to provide for their communities, treat workers fairly, and glorify the Lord through their success.

However, others, motivated by greed and self-interest, used the same advancements for selfish gain, exploiting workers and accumulating wealth without considering God's principles. This is not a condemnation of the **Industrial Revolution** itself, but a reflection on the power of **free will**. **Deuteronomy 30:19** reminds us, *"I have set before you life and death, blessings and curses. Now choose life, so that you and your children may live."* The choice has always been ours—to use God's gifts to **honor Him** or to satisfy our own desires. The technology and innovations provided by the Industrial Revolution were tools, but how we wield those tools depends on whether we choose to walk in the **fear of the Lord** and seek to **love and serve Him** above all else.

# Chapter 3

## Godly Heroes in the Industrial Revolution

During the Industrial Revolution, God raised up faithful servants who saw the exploitation of workers and felt called to action. These Christian reformers didn't just pray for change - they fought for it in Parliament, in prisons, in factories, and in the streets. Their stories show us how God works through ordinary people to protect the vulnerable and fight injustice. Let's meet some of these remarkable individuals who transformed their faith into action.

Here's a list of **Godly individuals** who worked hard during the **Industrial Revolution** to protect people from the evil and exploitation of those who chose to use the era's opportunities for selfish gain. Each of these people felt called by God to improve the lives of workers, fight for justice, and provide hope during a time of significant economic and social upheaval.

### 1. William Wilberforce

**Cause**: Social reform and the abolition of slavery

**What he did**: A British politician and devout Christian, **William Wilberforce** dedicated much of his life to fighting for the abolition of slavery and the improvement of workers' conditions during the Industrial Revolution. He was part of the **Clapham Sect**, a group of evangelical Christians who sought to apply Christian principles to social issues. In addition to leading the fight for the abolition of the British slave trade (achieved in 1807), Wilberforce also advocated for factory reform, improved working conditions, and the moral welfare of the poor. His tireless campaigning was driven by his deep Christian faith, believing that all humans are created in the image of God and deserve dignity. **Psalm 82:3** says, *"Defend the weak and the fatherless; uphold the cause of the poor and the oppressed."* Wilberforce embodied this verse in both his political work and personal life.

### 2. Lord Shaftesbury (Anthony Ashley-Cooper, 7th Earl of Shaftesbury)

**Cause**: Child labor reform and workers' rights

**What he did**: Known as the "Poor Man's Earl," **Lord Shaftesbury** was a Christian philanthropist and social reformer in 19th-century England. His Christian convictions led him to champion the cause of children who worked in factories and mines. **He passed the Factory Act of 1833**, which restricted child labor and improved working conditions. He also helped pass the **Mines Act of 1842**, which banned women and children from working in coal mines. Shaftesbury believed that his work was a **calling from God** and frequently referenced Scripture, such as **James 1:27**, *"Religion that God our Father accepts as pure and faultless is this: to look after orphans and widows in their distress and to keep oneself from being polluted by the world."* His dedication to helping the marginalized was motivated by his deep love for Jesus.

### 3. Elizabeth Fry

**Cause**: Prison reform and care for the poor

**What she did**: A Quaker Christian and social reformer, **Elizabeth Fry** is best known for her work in improving conditions in British prisons, particularly for women. While the Industrial Revolution caused massive changes in society, many people found themselves falling into poverty and crime due to harsh working conditions and low wages. Fry visited prisons where women and children were kept in appalling conditions and lobbied the government to improve these institutions. Her faith in God compelled her to fight for the dignity of all people. She believed in the biblical mandate to care for the **least of these** (Matthew 25:40), and she set up educational programs, provided medical care, and advocated for prison reform. Her compassionate approach earned her the respect of many, and she became one of the leading voices for prison reform during the 19th century.

### 4. George Müller

**Cause**: Orphan care and faith-based provision

**What he did**: **George Müller** was a Christian evangelist and director of orphanages in Bristol, England. As the Industrial Revolution drew people to cities, it also left many children orphaned, abandoned, or destitute. Müller felt called by God to provide for these children, and he did so entirely by faith. Without ever asking for donations, Müller opened orphanages and cared for more than 10,000 children during his lifetime. He trusted God for provision and was inspired by **Psalm 68:5**, which describes God as *"a father to the fatherless."* His deep reliance on prayer and faith provided shelter, education, and care to children left behind by society. His work stood as a powerful testament to God's provision and faithfulness, showing that even in the midst of hardship, God still cares for His people.

### 5. Robert Raikes

**Cause**: Founder of Sunday Schools

**What he did**: During the Industrial Revolution, many children worked long hours in factories and had little to no access to education. **Robert Raikes**, a British journalist and philanthropist, saw this and was inspired to provide education through **Sunday Schools**. These schools offered basic education in reading, writing, and religious instruction to poor working-class children who otherwise had no opportunity to learn. Raikes believed in the importance of teaching both literacy and the Bible, and he viewed education as a tool to break the cycle of poverty. **Proverbs 22:6** guided his mission: *"Train up a child in the way he should go; even when he is old he will not depart* *from it."* Raikes' Sunday School movement spread across the world and laid the foundation for modern public education systems.

### 6. Charles Spurgeon

**Cause**: Christian outreach and charity

**What he did**: **Charles Spurgeon**, one of the greatest preachers of the 19th century, was deeply concerned with the social and spiritual welfare of those impacted by the Industrial Revolution. Spurgeon, known as the "Prince of Preachers," led the **Metropolitan Tabernacle** in London and was actively involved in numerous **charities** aimed at helping the poor, the sick, and the orphaned. He established **orphanages**, supported workers' rights, and preached the importance of Christians caring for the least among them. His sermons often referenced passages like **Matthew 25:40**, where Jesus speaks of caring for "the least of these," reminding his congregation that Christian faith must lead to practical action. Spurgeon's compassionate approach to ministry made him a beacon of hope for many suffering under the hardships of industrialization.

### 7. John Wesley

**Cause**: Social reform, workers' rights, and spiritual revival

**What he did**: **John Wesley**, the founder of **Methodism**, was deeply involved in the social and spiritual issues that arose during the Industrial Revolution. He preached tirelessly across England, advocating for the **dignity of laborers** and the working class, who were often exploited in harsh working conditions. Wesley's sermons emphasized **social holiness**, which called for Christians to take an active role in transforming society by living out their faith through acts of justice and mercy. His influence extended to **early labor movements**, as he encouraged Methodists to help the poor and sick. Wesley's call for workers to find rest and renewal in Christ (Matthew 11:28-30) was a powerful counterbalance to the exhausting demands of the industrial workforce.

These men and women of faith were instrumental in **protecting and uplifting** those who were being mistreated during the Industrial Revolution. Their actions were not just **motivated by compassion** but also by **a deep commitment to God's Word**. They understood that **God's heart** is for justice, mercy, and the protection of the vulnerable, and they worked tirelessly to bring about change, even in the face of overwhelming challenges. Their legacies continue to inspire Christians today to be agents of change in their communities, living out the truth of **Micah 6:8**:

*"He has shown you, O mortal, what is good. And what does the Lord require of you? To act justly and to love mercy and to walk humbly with your God."*

Being a **hero of the faith**—standing up against the evil acts of the enemy—is of critical importance, especially during times like the **Industrial Revolution** when the vulnerable were often exploited, abused, and forgotten. In a period of rapid change, where greed and injustice easily crept in, God raised up men and women to **fight for the dignity and rights of workers**, who often didn't even realize the spiritual and social battles being waged on their behalf. The **enemy sought to destroy** lives through dangerous working conditions, unfair wages, and child labor, but God worked through faithful individuals who stood firm, protecting His people from the worst evils of that time. These heroes operated in the background, unseen by most, but their work saved lives, upheld justice, and demonstrated the heart of Christ for the oppressed. **Ephesians 6:12** reminds us that our battle is not against flesh and blood but against the rulers, authorities, and spiritual forces of evil, and these heroes of the faith were on the front lines of that battle.

For the **thousands of factory workers**, miners, and children who lived day by day under these newly formed laws, the impact was life-changing—even if they didn't always know it. A young boy working in a coal mine might not have known that, just a few years prior, he could have been forced to work for 16 hours a day, with no safety measures in place. A factory worker, though weary from long shifts, likely didn't know how reformers fought tirelessly for their right to shorter work hours, better pay, and safe environments. The battles fought by people like **Lord Shaftesbury** and **Elizabeth Fry** brought tangible relief to those who had been crushed under the weight of unchecked exploitation. These unsung individuals may never have heard the names of their advocates, but they felt the **blessings of their courage** every time they went home from work a little earlier or received wages that could finally support their families.

This protection meant more than just physical safety; it was also **spiritual care**. For the **day-to-day workers**, many of whom had little control over their circumstances, these reforms gave them **dignity** and a sense that someone cared—whether it was their fellow man or a higher power. The reforms that emerged, rooted in the **Christian principles of justice and mercy**, were a manifestation of God's protection over His people. Workers could live their lives with more **hope**, knowing they were no longer completely at the mercy of greedy factory owners or harsh conditions. In the midst of the industrial machines and the smoke-filled cities, God's hand was there, working through His people to provide a refuge in the midst of turmoil. These laws became a form of **God's justice on earth**, a reminder that His love extends to every person, in every factory, on every street, even when the enemy tries to bring harm.

While these reformers' names echo through history, their greatest impact was on countless unknown lives - people like Margaret Davies, whose story shows us how God's protection flows through the actions of His faithful servants to touch generations of families.

## Story Time: Heroes of the Faith in the Industrial Revolution

In the dim, hazy light of a Manchester textile mill, **Margaret Davies**, a thin, frail girl of only 12, bent over a loom, her hands raw from the coarse threads she had worked with since dawn. The machines roared around her, filling the air with a relentless hum that drowned out any thought of peace. Her days were long and exhausting, and the work was dangerous. Margaret had seen other children lose fingers to the machines or worse, but she had no choice. This mill was her family's only means of survival. What Margaret didn't know was that **God's unseen hand** had already begun to move in the hearts of faithful reformers—people whose names she would never hear but whose work would save her life and the lives of countless others.

Years earlier, the mill's conditions would have been far worse. Before the **Factory Acts** were passed, children worked up to 16 hours a day in filthy, airless rooms with no safety regulations. However, through the tireless efforts of Christian reformers like **Lord Shaftesbury**, **Elizabeth Fry**, and **Robert Raikes**, laws were passed that limited child labor and demanded safer working conditions. These reforms, born out of a deep conviction that every life mattered to God, had a profound impact on Margaret's life, though she never knew it. The simple fact that she could go home each night, battered and bruised but alive, was a direct result of the faithfulness of those who had **stood against the evils** of exploitation. **Psalm 82:3** came to life through their work: *"Defend the weak and the fatherless; uphold the cause of the poor and the oppressed."*

Margaret's story could have ended there, in that mill. Many children didn't survive the harsh conditions, and before the reforms, she might have been one of them. But God had other plans. She eventually left the mill, older and wiser, and found work as a seamstress. She met and married **Thomas Davies**, a factory worker, and together they began a new chapter in their lives. They struggled, but they were grateful. They could have been crushed by the weight of poverty and exploitation, but thanks to the reforms inspired by **God's justice**, they were able to build a modest yet secure life.

Margaret and Thomas had three children. Their oldest son, **John**, grew up hearing stories of the mill where his mother worked as a child, though she always spoke of it with a mixture of pain and gratitude. The mill had shaped her, yes, but she was alive because **someone had fought for her**—people she would never meet, but whom God had sent as **protectors and defenders**. John, inspired by the resilience of his mother and her faith in God, became a carpenter, building homes for families who, like his own, sought safety and shelter in an uncertain world. His hands, rough from years of working with wood, carried on the legacy of hard, honest work, but they also held a future that would have been unimaginable had his mother not survived those early years in the mill.

As the years went by, **John's own children** grew. His daughter, **Anne**, inherited her grandmother Margaret's fierce determination and her father's work ethic. Anne became a schoolteacher, educating the children of Manchester's working class. She knew that education was the key to breaking the cycle of poverty that had gripped her family for generations. She never forgot the stories of her grandmother's childhood, and she often told her students about the hard-won rights that allowed them to be in school rather than in factories. "You're here because someone fought for you," she would say. "People like **Lord Shaftesbury** and **Elizabeth Fry** didn't even know your names, but they fought for your future because they knew God cared about you."

Anne married **David**, a man who shared her passion for education and justice. Together, they raised a family, instilling in their children the values of hard work, faith, and compassion for others. Their youngest son, **George**, carried the torch of this legacy into the 20th century. George became a lawyer, driven by a deep sense of justice and the conviction that his work could make a difference. He specialized in workers' rights, defending those who were still being taken advantage of in the industrial landscape, which had evolved but was still fraught with inequality.

George's work, like that of his ancestors, was **rooted in faith**. He often thought of his great-grandmother Margaret, who had barely survived the dangers of the mill. He knew that without the reforms fought for by **heroes of the faith**, she might never have lived to see her children or grandchildren. Without those who had stood up against exploitation and fought for justice, George's very life might never have existed. **God had protected his family**, and now it was his turn to be that protector for others. His favorite Bible verse was **Micah 6:8**:

*"He has shown you, O mortal, what is good. And what does the Lord require of you? To act justly and to love mercy and to walk humbly with your God."* George lived this out every day in the courtroom, where he fought for the voiceless.

George married **Eleanor**, and together they raised three children, including their daughter **Emily**. By the time Emily was born in the 1970s, the world had changed dramatically, but the legacy of faith and justice that had been passed down through her family was stronger than ever. Emily became a doctor, using her skills to serve those who couldn't afford proper healthcare. Like her great-great-grandmother Margaret, Emily worked long hours, but in a much different environment. Margaret had fought to survive in a world that sought to use her up and cast her aside, while Emily was now in a position to **save lives**, offering healing to those in need.

One night, as Emily sat at her desk, reflecting on a long day in the hospital, she thought about the journey that had brought her here. She remembered the stories her father, George, had told her about their family's history—the mill where Margaret had worked, the reforms that had saved her life, and the heroes who had fought for people like her. Emily realized that **her life was a product of God's faithfulness**, passed down through generations. **The work of those long-forgotten heroes of the faith**—people like **Lord Shaftesbury**, **Elizabeth Fry**, and **George Müller**—had made it possible for her family to survive, thrive, and make a difference in the world.

What struck Emily most deeply was that the people who had fought for her great-great-grandmother **never knew her name**. They had no idea that their work would one day result in a doctor sitting in a London hospital in the year 2000, saving lives. Yet, **God knew**. He had seen Margaret, a scared little girl in a textile mill, and He had seen Emily, working in a hospital nearly two centuries later. **God's faithfulness had stretched across generations,** from the mills of the 1830s to the hospitals of the 21st century. The heroes of the faith who had stood up against injustice didn't just change laws—they changed

**lives**. They saved entire families, creating legacies that would ripple through history in ways no one could have imagined.

Emily realized that her family's story wasn't just about survival—it was about **God's providence**. He had placed people like **Margaret, John, Anne,** and **George** in a long line of faithful individuals who had responded to the **call of justice** and **compassion**. The work of those early reformers had protected Margaret, and because of that protection, **thousands of lives had been touched** through the generations that followed.

The legacy of faith, justice, and protection continued to flow through Emily's veins. She knew that **God saw** every act of faithfulness, even the ones that went unnoticed by the world. The heroes of the Industrial Revolution had fought for those who could not fight for themselves, and their legacy was now woven into the fabric of history, carried forward by people like Emily, who chose to serve and protect others in the name of Christ.

As Emily bowed her head in prayer that night, she thanked God for the heroes who had gone before her, for the legacy of faith that had been passed down through her family, and for the chance to continue the work of **God's kingdom**—to protect, to heal, and to love. She knew that the **story of God's faithfulness** was still unfolding, and she was honored to be a part of it.

## Redeeming Creation: God's Faithful Servants in a World of Brokenness

God has always been the **Creator of all good things**. His creation is filled with beauty, innovation, and purpose, all designed to **bless humanity** and reflect His glory. From the earliest days of humanity, **Genesis 1:31** reminds us, *"God saw all that He had made, and it was very good."* However, in a world where the **enemy seeks to corrupt** and destroy, there are countless examples of people being convinced to misuse the **gifts of God** for selfish gain or harm. The enemy, who is described in **John 10:10** as coming *"only to steal and kill and* *destroy,"* often manipulates and distorts what God created for good, leading to exploitation, injustice, and suffering.

Yet, **God's sovereignty** remains unshaken, even in a world where the enemy has temporary dominion. While Satan may try to twist God's creation, **God sends faithful servants** to redeem what has been broken. Time and time again, God raises up people to confront these abuses, restore justice, and reclaim His creation for His purposes. This is part of **God's ongoing fulfillment of His covenant** to care for His people and bring redemption to the world. **Romans 8:28** promises that God works *"for the good of those who love Him, who have been called according to His purpose."* When things go wrong, and humanity misuses the gifts God has given, He intervenes through His people to set things right again.

One profound example is obviously the **Industrial Revolution**. God blessed humanity with technological advancements like the **steam engine**, **textile machines**, and **railways**—inventions that were meant to ease burdens, create wealth, and provide for growing populations. However, the enemy twisted these blessings, convincing some to use them for **exploitation and greed**. Workers, including children, were forced into **dangerous conditions** for meager wages, while factory owners amassed wealth. But God, in His grace, sent **faithful reformers**—people like **Lord Shaftesbury**, **Elizabeth Fry**, and **William Wilberforce**—who saw the injustice and fought to **redeem the broken systems**. Through their efforts, **laws were changed**, and working conditions were improved, reflecting God's heart for justice and compassion. **Isaiah 1:17** says, *"Learn to do right; seek justice. Defend the oppressed."* These reformers were living out God's call to restore what the enemy had tried to corrupt.

This pattern of **redemption** happens repeatedly in our fallen world. Though **Satan may have temporary dominion**, as **2 Corinthians 4:4** describes him as the "god of this world," **God remains sovereign**. He continues to fulfill His covenant promises to bless and care for His people, despite the enemy's schemes. Whether it is through social reform, justice movements, or even the daily acts of kindness by believers, **God's faithful servants'** step into the gap to bring His light into the darkness. Even when we see the world's brokenness and the enemy's attempts to harm God's creation, we can trust that God is always working, sending His people to redeem and restore. **Revelation 21:5** declares, *"Behold, I am making all things new!"* God's heart is to redeem what has been lost, to bring healing to the broken, and to fulfill His promises of covenant love and care for His people.

In a world marred by sin and darkness, **God's faithfulness** never fades. As He continues to fulfill His covenants—promises made to **Abraham, Moses**, and through **Jesus Christ**—He uses **ordinary people** to do extraordinary things, **redeeming His creation** and reminding the world that His plans cannot be thwarted. **Psalm 33:11** proclaims, *"The plans of the Lord stand firm forever, the purposes of His heart through all generations."* No matter how much the enemy tries to corrupt, God will always have the final word.

# Chapter 4

# The Industrial Revolution as a Fulfillment of God's Covenant with His People

## The Industrial Revolution as a Fulfillment of God's Covenant with His People

The **Industrial Revolution**—an era of rapid innovation, economic growth, and social change—was not merely a human achievement but a **powerful example of God's covenantal faithfulness** being fulfilled throughout history. Originally, God's covenants were made specifically with the **Jewish people**—from Abraham to Moses and David—but through the **New Covenant in Christ**, these promises have been extended to **all believers**, both Jew and Gentile. As **Galatians 3:28** explains, *"There is neither Jew nor Greek, there is neither slave nor free, there is neither male nor female, for you are all one in Christ Jesus."* The Industrial Revolution can be viewed as a tangible expression of these covenant promises being fulfilled across all nations, as **God equipped humanity** with new tools to multiply resources, enhance productivity, and elevate entire nations. This period of history highlights how God, throughout the ages, has been faithfully working to provide for His people and fulfill His covenant, not only to the Jewish people but now to **all who believe** in Christ.

# The History of God's Covenants and Their Fulfillment

From the very beginning, God established **covenants** with His people, starting with the **Jewish people**, binding Himself to them in promises of provision, protection, and blessings. The first major covenant was made with **Abraham** in **Genesis 12:2-3**, where God promised,

*"I will make you into a great nation, and I will bless you; I will make your name great, and you will be a blessing. I will bless those who bless you, and whoever curses you I will curse; and all peoples on earth will be blessed through you."*

This covenant extended beyond Abraham and applied to his descendants, specifically the Jewish people, making them God's chosen nation. However, under the **New Covenant**, which was inaugurated through the death and resurrection of Jesus Christ, **all believers are now partakers of this promise**. **Romans 10:12** states, *"For there is no difference between Jew and Gentile—the same Lord is Lord of all and richly blesses all who call on Him."* Through Jesus, the covenant promises have been opened to all who believe, making every believer—whether Jew or Gentile—an heir to these blessings.

Following the Abrahamic Covenant, God continued to establish **new covenants** with His people—such as the **Mosaic Covenant**, where He gave the Law to guide the Israelites, and later the **Davidic Covenant**, where He promised that a descendant of David would reign forever. Each of these covenants was given to the Jewish people, but they also laid the foundation for the **New Covenant in Christ**, where believers from every nation are now given **full access to God's promises** through faith in Jesus. **Jeremiah 31:31-33** foretells this New Covenant, where God promises to write His law on the hearts of His people, not just the Jews but **all believers**, and to bless them with a personal, intimate relationship with Him.

# Inheritance of Believers: Partakers of the Covenants

Through Jesus Christ, **all believers have become heirs** to the covenantal promises originally given to the Jewish people. **Galatians 3:29** makes it clear: *"If you belong to Christ, then you are Abraham's seed, and heirs according to the promise."* This means that Christians today are part of this **spiritual and material inheritance**—the blessings God promised to Abraham and his descendants now belong to us through faith in Christ. These promises include not only spiritual blessings but also material and physical provisions, as seen throughout the Old Testament. For instance, God promised **land, prosperity, and protection** under the Abrahamic, Mosaic, and Davidic Covenants.

In the **Abrahamic Covenant**, God promised to make Abraham's descendants as numerous as the stars and to give them the **land of Canaan** (Genesis 17:7-8). Under the **Mosaic Covenant**, God promised that if His people obeyed His commandments, He would **bless their land**, multiply their harvests, and give them **peace** (Deuteronomy 28:1-14). The **Davidic Covenant** promised a **lasting kingdom**, fulfilled ultimately in Jesus, who reigns eternally. In the **New Covenant**, these promises are spiritualized but also manifest in practical ways. God provides for His people, now extended to all believers, through His **blessings of provision, protection, and prosperity**. As believers, we inherit **God's covenant blessings**, such as provision (Matthew 6:33), protection (Psalm 91), and spiritual prosperity (John 10:10).

As believers, we can see the **Industrial Revolution** as Part of God's fulfillment of these promises. He provided new technologies, such as the **spinning jenny**, **steam engines**, and **power looms**, which allowed His people to multiply their resources and improve their livelihoods. This explosion of productivity was not just for personal gain but was meant to **bless the nations**, aligning with the promise made to Abraham that *"all peoples on earth will be blessed through you"* (Genesis 12:3).

Let's see how these promises played out in real life during the Industrial Revolution. When a farmer could suddenly produce more food using new machinery, that was God fulfilling His promise of provision. When factories created jobs that lifted families out of poverty, that was God kept His covenant to bless His people. These technological advances were God's promises coming true in practical ways.

## The Industrial Revolution: A Manifestation of God's Provision

The Industrial Revolution was a **visible manifestation of God's provision**. For centuries, many people labored under difficult conditions, barely producing enough food and goods to sustain themselves. But God, in His perfect timing, began to unlock **new levels of innovation** that transformed the way humanity worked. It was as if the **windows of heaven** were opened, allowing people to discover new ways to create and produce.

God's covenant with Abraham included a promise of **land and prosperity**—and we can see this echoed in the Industrial Revolution, where nations expanded their capabilities to produce wealth, commerce, and goods. The advancements during this time were a **blessing** to millions, as people were lifted out of poverty, nations grew wealthier, and more people were able to **enjoy the fruits of creation**. God had promised in **Deuteronomy 28:11** that if His people followed Him, He would *"grant you abundant prosperity—in the fruit of your womb, the young of your livestock and the crops of your ground—in the land He swore to your ancestors to give you."* While this was initially given to the Jewish people, we now see these promises fulfilled on a global scale, as **all believers** around the world benefited from the Industrial Revolution.

# The Continuation of God's Faithfulness into the 1700s

Even though the **covenants** were made thousands of years before the Industrial Revolution, God's promises never faltered. **Isaiah 55:11** reminds us that God's word *"will not return to me empty but will accomplish what I desire and achieve the purpose for which I sent it."* The advancements made in the 1700s were a direct result of **God's ongoing faithfulness** to fulfill His covenant, not just to the Jewish people but now to all who call upon His name. The same God who gave wisdom to **Joseph** to store grain in Egypt during a famine was the God who gave wisdom to inventors like **James Watt**, **Richard Arkwright**, and **George Stephenson**. Their inventions—the steam engine, the spinning frame, and the locomotive—were more than just innovations; they were tools that **God used to fulfill His covenant promises** of provision and blessing to all believers.

By the 1700s, God had already established His pattern of blessing His people through innovation. The Industrial Revolution can be seen as a continuation of **God's abundant provision**, as He used human ingenuity to further His purposes. **Proverbs 8:12** says, *"I, wisdom, dwell with prudence, and I find knowledge and discretion."* It was this divine wisdom that enabled humanity to discover new ways to work, produce, and create. These innovations allowed people to experience **God's covenant blessings** in a fresh, tangible way, no longer just limited to the land of Israel but extending to **all corners of the earth**.

# God's Covenant and the Future: He Is Still Fulfilling His Promises

Even now, **God continues to fulfill His covenant with His people**. The advancements we enjoy today—whether through technology, medicine, or economics—are part of **His ongoing faithfulness** to bless and provide for us, regardless of whether we are Jew or Gentile. **Psalm 105:8** says, *"He remembers His covenant forever, the promise He made, for a thousand generations."* The Industrial Revolution was a part of God's plan, but it was not the end. He continues to pour out blessings on those who walk in His ways, and the prosperity seen in the 1700s was just one example of this.

The exciting truth is that **God is not finished yet**! The same God who provided for Abraham, Moses, David, and the early Church is providing for us today. The **Industrial Revolution** was one chapter in the unfolding story of God's covenant faithfulness, and we are living in the continuation of that story. Just as He blessed the nations through the Industrial Revolution, He continues to bless us with new technologies, industries, and innovations that bring prosperity and advance His Kingdom.

We are part of **God's covenant inheritance**, and the blessings He promised thousands of years ago are still being fulfilled today. Whether through the **Industrial Revolution** or the latest advancements in technology, God is working to fulfill His promises, bless His people, and bring glory to His name. **The covenant is alive, and God is always faithful**—both to the **Jewish people**, who were the original recipients of His promises and to all who have come to faith through Christ, for we are now **one in Him**.

# Conclusion: The Call to Step into God's Sovereign Plan

Exploitation and Inequality: The Dark Side of the Industrial Revolution"

As we reflect on the Industrial Revolution, we see why this history matters today. Throughout that era, God blessed humanity with incredible innovations, empowering people with knowledge and creativity to revolutionize industry. These advancements created jobs, provided for families, and brought economic growth. Today, we see the same pattern with modern technology. Just as God brought wisdom to transform manufacturing and commerce in the 1700s, He now provides new digital tools to connect and empower His people. The internet, like the steam engine before it, represents God's covenant promise of provision in action. And like the Industrial Revolution, it shows how the enemy tries to corrupt God's gifts - but God's purposes always prevail.

Just as God brought wisdom and direction to His people during the Industrial Revolution, blessing them through covenant innovation, we see the same pattern today with the internet. The internet, another incredible tool of innovation, is a modern example of God's blessings meant to connect, uplift, and bless His people. Through this vast network of information, communication, and opportunity, God has opened doors for sharing the Gospel, building community, and enabling businesses to thrive in ways once unimaginable. It is His covenant promise in action, using technology to bless and provide for His people. Yet, the enemy is once again at work, attempting to corrupt this blessing. The internet has also become a battleground, where deception, exploitation, and sin are rampant. Just as greed and abuse marked the Industrial Revolution, today we see the enemy twisting the internet into a tool for division, misinformation, and the enslavement of minds through addictive and harmful content.

But God's wisdom is always at work, guiding His people to use the internet for good and to expose the enemy's schemes. We are called to be lights in the digital world, bringing truth, grace, and integrity into spaces that have been darkened by corruption. We can make a difference by using this tool in ways that glorify God—spreading His Word, protecting the vulnerable, and standing against the forces of greed and deceit. By following His wisdom, we can reclaim the internet as the blessing it was intended to be and bring glory to God in this technological age, just as He did through the innovations of the past. Let us rise with courage, recognize the pattern, stand firm, and know that God's plans cannot be thwarted and that His blessings will always prevail.

As we come to the end of **Part 1: Creation and Innovation Under God's Sovereignty**, take a moment to reflect on the incredible journey we've explored together. We've seen how God, the ultimate Creator, not only shaped the world through His Word but also continues to move through human innovation, especially in the modern era. The breathtaking advancements in technology, like the internet, and artificial intelligence, and even historical milestones like the Industrial Revolution, are not random achievements—they are direct reflections of God's divine wisdom and plan.

This isn't just an abstract idea. Let's go back to the story of John, Sarah, and Matthew, ordinary people whose lives were transformed by the inventions and opportunities God brought into the world. Imagine John standing in awe as the spinning jenny spun threads faster than he could have ever managed by hand or Sarah's joy when her family finally had enough to eat because the factory work allowed her to bring home a livable wage. These were not just coincidences; they were moments where God was showing His provision, His care, and His desire to use even the seemingly mundane innovations to bring blessings into our lives.

Their stories show us how God used innovation to transform lives. Today, we see similar transformations through technology. A freelancer supporting their family through online work, a small business owner reaching customers globally, a teacher connecting with students worldwide, these are modern John's, Sarah's, and Matthew's, experiencing God's provision through new tools.

However, John, Sarah, and Matthew are not passive in this story. They chose to step forward, to trust in God's provision, and to use the tools He had given them for good. This is where you come in. As you reflect on the truths presented in this first part, you are invited to do the same. God has given you talents, gifts, and even access to technology that can be used for His glory. You have a role in this master plan—a plan that extends beyond just using technology, but in reclaiming it for God's Kingdom.

## What Will You Do Next?

As you move forward, know that there is more to discover. Part 2 will take us deeper into **The Journey of Tenacity: Trusting God's Path**

**to a Life Overflowing with Blessings.** We will uncover not just how God blesses us through creation and innovation, but how He calls us to persevere, to trust Him when life gets tough, and to recognize that every trial, every challenge, is part of a grander design for abundance and blessing.

The battle for your digital soul, as introduced in the beginning, is ongoing. The enemy doesn't rest. But neither does God. He is constantly equipping you, and the tools, strategies, and divine protection He has provided are only the beginning. Do you feel that stirring inside? That's God calling you to press on, to move from just understanding to actively participating in His plan.

## A Personal Challenge

I challenge you to look at your own life. What tools, technologies, or resources are at your disposal right now that you could reclaim for God's glory? It could be as simple as how you use your phone, the websites you visit, or the digital conversations you have. Are you using these tools to advance God's kingdom, or are they distractions pulling you away from His purpose?

Imagine how much more fulfilling life could be if, like John, Sarah, and Matthew, you step into the abundance God is offering. Picture yourself looking back, knowing that you were part of something bigger than you could have ever dreamed—God's sovereign plan in action.

## Moving Forward

So, as we close this chapter, take the leap of faith. Step into **Part 2:** with confidence and ˙excitement, knowing that God has already equipped you for the battles ahead. You're not just reading a book— you're being prepared for the next stage of your life, a stage where you are empowered to use all that God has given you to live a life overflowing with His blessings.

**Will you answer the call?** Let's continue this journey together. Let's reclaim the digital world and every other resource God has placed in our hands for His glory. The next chapter is waiting for you. The battle is real, but so is the victory. Let's move forward with tenacity, faith, and a heart fully surrendered to God's incredible plan.

**Get ready for Part 2—it's time to fight, to persevere, and to thrive.**

# Part 2

# Divine Innovation: The Rise of Computers and Software as Tools of God's Plan

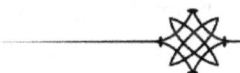

# How God Orchestrated the Birth of Computing to Empower Humanity and Fulfill His Purposes Through Technology

Welcome to Part 2: *Divine Innovation: The Rise of Computers and Software as Tools of God's Plan.* This section takes you on a journey through history, uncovering the divine orchestration behind one of humanity's greatest breakthroughs—the birth of computing. As you dive into these chapters, you'll discover how God has worked through inventors, mathematicians, and engineers to bring forth computers and software, equipping humanity with tools to solve problems, communicate globally, and fulfill His purposes. Far from being a product of human intellect alone, computing reflects God's wisdom and creativity, guiding us into an era of technological advancement that aligns with His grand design. Prepare to be inspired by how this innovation is not just changing our world but playing a pivotal role in God's plan for humanity.

# Chapter 5

## Divine Innovation: The Rise of Computers and Software as Tools of God's Plan

### The Development of Computers: The Next Wave of Innovation using Divine Hand in the Birth of Computing

As the **Industrial Revolution** drew to a close and the 20th century began, the world stood on the brink of the next major technological leap: the development of **computers**. These machines would revolutionize the way people processed information, communicated, and solved problems. While the industrial age had brought us steam engines, factories, and railways, the birth of computing would usher in an era of **information technology** that would forever change human society. I believe that, just as God guided the advancements of the **Industrial Revolution**, He was deeply involved in the birth and development of computers, giving key thinkers the **wisdom and insight** to create systems that would have a lasting impact on the world.

The concept of a mechanical device that could perform calculations can be traced back to **Charles Babbage** in the 1830s. Babbage, an English mathematician and inventor, designed the **Analytical Engine**, a mechanical general-purpose computer capable of performing any calculation, given the right instructions. Though his design was never fully realized during his lifetime due to technological limitations, his visionary work laid the foundation for modern computing. **God's providence** is evident in Babbage's life, as he was given the insight to see beyond the tools of his time and envision a machine that would revolutionize the future. While Babbage may never have seen his ideas brought to life, his work is a testament to **God's orchestration** in human creativity and innovation. As **Proverbs 16:9** says, *"In their hearts humans plan their course, but the Lord establishes their steps."*

Fast forward to the mid-20th century, and the world found itself in the midst of **World War II**, where the need for advanced computational power was urgent. Enter **Alan Turing**, often considered the father of modern computing. Turing's work on cryptography during the war led to the development of machines that helped the **Allied forces** break the German **Enigma code**, a feat that significantly aided in their victory. Turing's work didn't stop there; he also introduced the concept of a "universal machine"—what we now call a **computer**—that could solve any problem given the right instructions. His pioneering theories of computation introduced the idea of using **algorithms** to solve complex problems, laying the groundwork for how computers operate today. Though Turing faced immense personal and societal challenges, his contributions were crucial, and it's hard not to see **God's guiding hand** in his work. **Isaiah 55:8-9** reminds us, *"For my thoughts are not your thoughts, neither are your ways my ways,"* and it seems that God was preparing the world for something far greater than anyone could have imagined.

The rapid development of computing continued after the war. In the 1940s, **John von Neumann**, a brilliant mathematician, proposed the architecture that would become the foundation for modern computers. The **von Neumann architecture**, as it became known, allowed computers to store both data and programs in memory, enabling them to execute complex instructions. This architecture remains the basis of how most computers operate today. **God's influence** is evident in von Neumann's work, as his design enabled computers to evolve into powerful machines that could perform everything from basic calculations to complex simulations. Von Neumann's architecture introduced the use of **binary code**—a system of 1s and 0s that serves as the language of computers. This simple yet elegant method of encoding information reflects the **order and precision** that God has built into the universe. **Colossians 1:16-17** says, *"For by Him all things were created, in heaven and on earth, visible and invisible... and in Him all things hold together."* God's orderly creation is mirrored in the precise and structured nature of computing, where even the most complex tasks can be broken down into simple binary instructions.

## How Computers Work: A Simple Explanation with Divine Insight

At their core, computers are machines designed to **process information** and execute instructions. These instructions come in the form of **programs** or **software**, which tell the computer how to perform specific tasks. Understanding how a computer works can be broken down into a few key components:

1. **Central Processing Unit (CPU)**: Often referred to as the "brain" of the computer, the CPU carries out the instructions given by the software. It processes data, performs calculations, and makes decisions based on the input it receives. The CPU operates at incredibly high speeds, executing millions or even billions of instructions per second.
2. **Memory (RAM)**: Random **Access Memory (RAM)** is where the computer temporarily stores data that the CPU needs to access quickly. It's like the computer's short-term memory,

helping it handle multiple tasks at once by keeping the necessary data readily available. When you open a program or file on your computer, it is loaded into RAM so that the CPU can quickly retrieve and process the information.

3. **Storage (Hard Drive or SSD)**: Computers also need a place to store information permanently, which is where the **hard drive** or **solid-state drive (SSD)** comes in. This is the long-term memory of the computer, where all the files, programs, and operating systems are stored when they are not in use. Unlike RAM, which is erased when the computer is turned off, data stored on the hard drive or SSD remains until it is deleted.

4. **Input/Output Devices**: These are the tools we use to communicate with the computer. **Input devices** like keyboards, mice, and touchscreens allow users to send data to the computer, while **output devices** like monitors and printers display the results of the computer's processing.

5. **Software**: While the hardware forms the physical structure of the computer, **software** provides the instructions. Software includes everything from the operating system (like **Windows** or **macOS**) to applications like word processors, web browsers, and games. **God's gift of creativity** is evident in the development of software, which allows computers to perform a virtually limitless range of tasks.

When a computer is powered on, the CPU immediately begins executing instructions, starting with the **operating system**, which manages all the other programs and resources. As users input data, the CPU processes it, retrieves necessary information from **RAM** or the **storage drive**, and outputs the results in a matter of milliseconds. Computers can perform **billions of calculations** per second, enabling them to solve problems, simulate environments, and perform tasks that would take humans a lifetime to accomplish. **Psalm 139:14** says, *"I praise you because I am fearfully and wonderfully made; your works are wonderful, I know that full well."* The intricate design of computing systems reflects the **intelligent design** we see in nature, and God's wisdom is evident in the remarkable complexity of these machines.

While Babbage, Turing, and von Neumann laid the technical foundation for computing, the real transformation happened when these machines entered our homes and changed our daily lives. My own journey from skeptic to believer mirrors how many people first encountered this new technology.

## From Floppy Disks to the Digital Age: My Journey into the World of Computers

It's amazing how far technology has come, but I still vividly remember the early days when computers first entered our homes. It felt like the dawn of a new era, though at the time, I couldn't have grasped the extent of its impact. Some people jumped into the digital age with both feet, ready to embrace whatever it had to offer. My brother was one of them—his excitement was unmatched. He saw the future in those mysterious machines, while I watched from a distance, unsure if this "computer craze" would be just another passing fad.

I remember the day he convinced our dad to spend what felt like an outrageous amount of money on what seemed to me like a glorified white box with a small TV screen attached. I didn't get it. I'd sit back and observe as they enthusiastically fed floppy disks into a slot in the machine, waiting with bated breath as the screen flickered to life with scrolling numbers and text. But for the life of me, I couldn't figure out what all the excitement was about. What were they seeing that I wasn't? To me, it was just a lot of flashing words with no discernible meaning.

At the time, I was still in high school, and there was an elective course called "Computers." Maybe, I thought, if I took that class, I'd finally understand the magic they were experiencing. I figured if nothing else, I could help my dad and brother figure out how to make that expensive white box do something useful. Looking back, I realize they didn't really know much more about it than I did—they were just fascinated by the potential.

So, I signed up for the class, hoping to crack the code. The first thing I learned was the terminology. It wasn't just a "white box"—it was a CPU. And the "small TV" was actually a monitor. The floppy disks were categorized as either storage disks to hold data or program disks that contained the software. For a semester, I immersed myself in this new digital language, trying to understand how it all worked.

But even after months of learning how to operate these strange machines, I still couldn't see what the big deal was. Why was everyone saying that computers would one day run the world? My final exam in that class involved writing a basic program to make my name repeat in a column on the screen repeatedly. It felt underwhelming, to say the least.

Yet here we are today. What started as an incomprehensible white box and a few floppy disks has evolved into the digital age that has transformed every facet of life. Back then, I couldn't have imagined that those clunky machines would lead to the world we live in now, where technology drives everything from communication to business, healthcare, and even entertainment. We've come so far, and sometimes I still find myself in awe of how much it has all changed.

## The Role of God in Orchestrating the Birth of Computing

The **birth of computing** was not merely a product of human ingenuity but a direct result of **God's orchestration** in human history. From Babbage's early mechanical designs to the powerful digital computers of today, **God's hand** has been guiding the process, preparing the world for a future where computing would play a crucial role. Just as God gave **wisdom to Solomon** to lead His people and build His temple, He gave wisdom to the early pioneers of computing to build machines that would change the world. **Proverbs 2:6** tells us, *"For* *the Lord gives wisdom; from His mouth comes knowledge and understanding."*

Through the development of computing, God laid the groundwork for the digital age—a time when information could be processed, stored, and shared with unprecedented speed and efficiency. Computers have transformed industries, revolutionized communication, and provided solutions to some of the world's most complex problems. But this is just the beginning of **God's plan**. The birth of computing has set the stage for even greater advancements, as we move into the **age of the internet**, where computers would become interconnected, creating a global network of information and communication.

As we transition into the next section, focusing on the development of the **internet**, we can see how **God's sovereignty** over technology continues to unfold. Just as He orchestrated the birth of computing, He has been guiding the evolution of the **digital age**, ensuring that these tools are used for His glory and the fulfillment of His purposes. While the enemy may try to twist and misuse technology for evil, **God remains in control**, working all things together for good.

## The History and Development of Networks: God's Creative Power Revealed

Networks, as we know them today, are the foundational technology that makes global communication, business, and digital life possible. The development of networks is a testament to God's creative power and His master plan to enable humanity to connect, share knowledge, and grow together. Just as the Industrial Revolution transformed industries and economies through innovation and collaboration, the development of digital networks has revolutionized the way people interact, share information, and build relationships. Networks, in many ways, represent God's desire for humanity to work together, share resources, and advance His kingdom.

# Early History: How Networks Came to Be

The history of networks dates back to the late 1960s when the U.S. Department of Defense developed the **Advanced Research Projects Agency Network (ARPANET)**. This was the first operational packet-switching network and is considered the precursor to the modern internet. The purpose of ARPANET was to create a decentralized communication system that could withstand failures or attacks, ensuring that vital communication could continue even if part of the system was damaged.

Key individuals involved in the development of ARPANET included **Paul Baran**, a researcher at the RAND Corporation, who proposed the concept of **packet switching**, and **Leonard Kleinrock**, a computer scientist at UCLA, who played a pivotal role in the mathematical theory of data networks. **Vinton Cerf** and **Robert Kahn** later contributed to the development of **TCP/IP** protocols, which enabled different networks to communicate with one another, laying the foundation for the global internet we use today.

Packet switching, the core concept behind ARPANET, allowed data to be broken down into smaller packets, sent independently through the network and reassembled at the destination. This decentralized approach ensured that if one route was compromised, data could be rerouted through other available paths. The genius of this concept reflects God's creative brilliance, showing us how seemingly complex problems can have elegant solutions when approached with wisdom and collaboration.

While ARPANET was initially developed for military use, its success quickly spread to academic and research institutions, where scientists and scholars could share data and collaborate on projects in real time. This interconnectedness mirrored the body of Christ, where each part has its own unique function, but all parts are interconnected and essential to the whole (1 Corinthians 12:12). In the same way, early networks connected different computers and systems, enabling them to work together toward common goals.

# The Growth of Networks and Early Challenges

As ARPANET grew, it became clear that the potential of networks extended far beyond military and academic use. By the 1970s and 1980s, research institutions, universities, and eventually corporations began adopting similar networking systems. The **Transmission Control Protocol/Internet Protocol (TCP/IP)** became the standard for network communication, allowing different networks to connect and share information.

However, the early days of networking were not without challenges. Networks were often unreliable, and data transmission was slow and prone to errors. Early adopters faced frequent failures due to technical limitations and underdeveloped infrastructure. But, just as in the Industrial Revolution, where inventors faced many setbacks before breakthroughs emerged, the perseverance of early network developers led to solutions that transformed these early struggles into lasting success.

In the Industrial Revolution, there were failures, challenges, and obstacles that innovators like James Watt, who improved the steam engine, and Eli Whitney, who invented the cotton gin, had to overcome. Similarly, in the development of digital networks, early challenges were met with innovation and collaboration. The eventual success of networks can be seen as a reflection of God's provision and creativity. Proverbs 16:3 tells us, "Commit to the Lord whatever you do, and He will establish your plans." Through perseverance and collaboration, networks evolved from rudimentary connections to the powerful, reliable systems we rely on today.

# The Value of Networks and God's Master Plan

At their core, networks are systems designed to connect. Whether it's two computers in a room or millions of devices across the globe, the value of networks lies in their ability to bring people, ideas, and resources together. In God's master plan, we see His intention for humanity to be connected, to share knowledge, and to work in harmony. Just as in the body of Christ, where every believer is a vital part of the whole (Romans 12:4-5), networks allow for each device, system, and person to contribute to a larger purpose.

In Ephesians 4:16, Paul describes how the whole body, "joined and held together by every supporting ligament, grows and builds itself up in love, as each part does its work." This is a powerful analogy for the way networks work. Each device or system on a network plays a specific role, but all are interconnected, sharing data and resources to accomplish greater goals. Whether it's facilitating communication, powering industries, or enabling scientific research, networks represent God's design for collaboration and growth.

## How Networks Work: A Simplified View

At a basic level, a **network** is a collection of devices—computers, servers, smartphones, routers—that are connected to one another, allowing them to communicate and share resources. These devices are linked either through **wired connections** (such as Ethernet cables) or **wireless connections** (such as Wi-Fi). Each device on the network is assigned a unique identifier called an **IP address**, which enables it to send and receive data.

Data sent across a network is broken into smaller pieces called **packets**. These packets travel across the network, hopping from device to device until they reach their destination. Once all the packets have arrived, they are reassembled to form the complete data (such as a file, video, or webpage). This process ensures that data can travel quickly and efficiently across networks, even if some parts of the network experience failures.

One of the most powerful aspects of networks is that they can scale infinitely. Just as a human body can grow stronger and more capable over time, networks can expand to include millions or even billions of devices. This scalability reflects God's creative power, which is limitless and infinite. Psalm 147:5 says, "Great is our Lord and mighty in power; His understanding has no limit." In the same way, the growth and potential of networks seem boundless, showcasing God's wisdom and brilliance in design.

## Discovering the Power of Networks: My First Glimpse into the Future of Computers

I still remember sitting in that college classroom, surrounded by rows of computers, each one perched neatly on flat desks where typewriters had once sat in my high school typing class. The room had about 50 computers, and the school was incredibly proud of their new "computer lab," as they called it. It was the latest innovation, and I felt like I was at the forefront of something new, though I wasn't quite sure what it was yet.

At that point, I didn't fully understand what computers were capable of, let alone what a network was, though the concept had not yet been introduced to us by that name. It wasn't until one particular class that I had my first "wow" moment with computers.

We were sitting in this large computer lab, and the instructor asked the person in the front row on the right side of the room to type a message on their computer and hit enter. We all sat there, waiting for something to happen. After a brief pause, the instructor then addressed the student sitting in the back row on the opposite side of the room, asking him what was displayed on his screen. To our amazement, he read aloud the exact message the first student had written.

There was a collective gasp. The girl in the front row couldn't believe it either—how had her message traveled from her computer to his? The instructor then told us that this was the future of communication: we would soon be able to send messages instantly from one person to another, no matter the distance. At that moment, I began to see a glimmer of the immense potential computers had to reshape how we interacted with the world.

Looking back now, I realize that what I had witnessed was an early version of networking. While we didn't use the term "network" back then, that's exactly what it was. These were the early days of local area networks (LANs), a technology that was quickly evolving to allow computers to communicate with each other.

The technology we were using in that classroom was still in its infancy, but it was enough to make me reconsider my skepticism. Could computers really change the way we send and receive messages? It seemed possible—perhaps they could even replace the postal service, I thought, given how quickly information had traveled across the room. Little did I know then that what I had just witnessed was the first step toward the world we live in today, where emails, instant messaging, and vast global networks are commonplace.

Back then, my understanding of the scope of this technology was still limited, but that classroom experience was a turning point. It planted the seed that would eventually grow into an awareness of just how integral computers—and their networks—would become to everyday life. It wasn't just about typing out messages anymore; this was about the dawn of a connected world.

## The Spiritual Significance of Networks

From a spiritual perspective, networks reflect the interconnectedness of humanity. We are all part of God's greater plan, and just as networks rely on communication and connection, so do we. The Bible emphasizes the importance of fellowship, unity, and collaboration. In Hebrews 10:24-25, we are encouraged to "consider how we may spur one another on toward love and good deeds, not giving up meeting together, as some are in the habit of doing, but encouraging one another."

In the same way, networks allow people across the world to connect, collaborate, and build communities. Whether it's connecting remote workers, enabling education in distant regions, or providing platforms for ministry and evangelism, networks have become a powerful tool for fulfilling God's purposes. God's master plan involves connecting

His people, and networks are one of the ways in which this divine connectivity is manifested in the modern world.

# God's Creative Power in the Development of Networks

Just as the Industrial Revolution was a period of rapid innovation and growth, the development of networks showcases God's creative power at work in human history. Networks allow for an unprecedented level of collaboration and connection, enabling people to achieve more together than they could on their own. This mirrors God's design for humanity: to live in community, support one another, and use the gifts He has given us for His glory.

Psalm 104:24 praises God's creation, saying, "How many are your works, Lord! In wisdom, you made them all; the earth is full of your creatures." Networks, like many technological advancements, are part of the wisdom and creativity that God has given to humanity. By developing networks, we are reflecting God's own creative nature and participating in His plan to bring people together for the common good.

## Conclusion: The Value of Networks in God's Plan

In conclusion, the development of networks is a clear example of God's provision and creative power at work in the world. From the early successes and failures of ARPANET to the vast, global networks we use today, the evolution of this technology mirrors God's design for humanity to be connected, collaborative, and innovative. Just as in the body of Christ, where each part plays an essential role in the health of the whole, networks bring value by connecting devices, people, and resources in a way that enables growth, communication, and shared purpose.

God's master plan has always been about connection—between Himself and His people, and between people and one another. Networks are one of the modern manifestations of this divine desire for connectivity, and they reveal God's brilliance and creativity in allowing humanity to grow and flourish in new ways. As we continue to develop and use networks, we are participating in God's plan, building the infrastructure that allows for knowledge, innovation, and fellowship to thrive across the globe.

## The Internet and Networks: A Story of God's Faithfulness and Human Innovation

The development of both **networks** and the **internet** are two of the most remarkable technological advancements in human history, each playing a critical role in how the world communicates, shares information, and connects today. While these innovations may seem like products of human ingenuity, they also reflect God's providential plan for humanity. Both networks and the internet have become tools that enable God's Word to be spread globally, uniting believers and advancing His Kingdom. But how did they come about, and how do they differ?

## The Birth of Networks: Laying the Foundation

Before the internet could revolutionize the world, the foundational technology of **networking** had to be developed. As we have learned A **network** is a system of interconnected computers and devices that can communicate and share resources, allowing for the exchange of data. This fundamental concept emerged in the 1960s when researchers and scientists were tasked with creating systems that could share data across different locations.

The creation of networks reflected God's design for humanity's interconnectedness. Just as networks allow computers and systems to share resources and information, God designed people to live in community, sharing knowledge and supporting one another. 1 Corinthians 12:12 teaches, "For just as the body is one and has many members, and all the members of the body, though many, are one body, so it is with Christ." Networks mirror this interconnectedness—

each part (or device) plays a vital role in the whole system, just as each believer contributes to the body of Christ.

## The Internet: A Network of Networks

While networks function locally, connecting a group of devices within a defined area (such as a home or an office), the **internet** is a **global network of interconnected networks**. It allows computers from all over the world to communicate with each other, regardless of their location. In essence, the internet is made up of thousands of smaller networks linked together by the **TCP/IP protocols**, which were developed during the early networking experiments like ARPANET.

The internet, as we know it today, began to take shape in the 1980s and 1990s. **Tim Berners-Lee** developed the **World Wide Web** in the early 1990s, creating a system of linked hypertext documents that could be accessed through web browsers. His work allowed for the easy sharing of information and enabled the average person to access vast amounts of data through user-friendly interfaces.

While the internet and networks function independently, they also work together. A **network** operates within a closed system, such as an office network connecting computers and printers. However, when that network is connected to the **internet**, it gains access to an entire world of information, services, and resources. Without networks, the internet wouldn't exist, and without the internet, networks would remain isolated.

## God's Hand in the Creation of Networks and the Internet

Just as God inspired the great inventors of the Industrial Revolution to create tools that would transform industries and improve human life, so too has He guided the development of networks and the internet. Networks made it possible for people to communicate over long distances, share knowledge, and collaborate on global projects. The internet expanded this potential exponentially, allowing information to flow freely across borders and oceans.

God's creative power is evident in the complexity and functionality of these technologies. While man may have discovered the methods to build these systems, the ability to create, think, and innovate comes from God alone. Proverbs 2:6 says, "For the Lord gives wisdom; from His mouth comes knowledge and understanding." God provided wisdom and understanding to those involved in developing these technologies, enabling them to create systems that would ultimately serve His greater plan for humanity.

## Early Challenges and Breakthroughs

As with any great technological advancement, the development of networks and the internet was not without challenges. In the early stages, networks were often unreliable. Data transmission was slow, and the infrastructure was prone to failure. However, just as the pioneers of the Industrial Revolution persevered through challenges to develop inventions like the steam engine and the spinning jenny, the creators of ARPANET and the internet faced their setbacks with determination. These early failures were critical learning experiences that eventually led to the breakthrough technologies we use today.

The eventual success of these systems highlights the perseverance and collaboration of the people involved, as well as God's guiding hand throughout the process. Romans 8:28 tells us, "And we know that in all things God works for the good of those who love Him, who have been called according to His purpose." The initial failures were part of a larger process, leading to the development of technologies that would allow for global communication, the spread of knowledge, and the advancement of God's Kingdom.

# Lost on the Information Highway: My Confusing Journey into the Early Internet

I remember my own bewildering journey trying to understand what the internet was—it felt like everyone had a vague answer, but none of it made sense to me. It was like chasing after an elusive concept that people seemed to understand, yet every explanation left me even more confused.

People kept telling me that the internet was like a "highway." That was the metaphor I heard the most—this "information highway" where you could find anything. I'd ask them, "Okay, but where's the onramp? How do I get on this highway?" They'd laugh and say I just needed to connect. But how? Where was this onramp they kept talking about? Once I was on this so-called highway, where exactly was I supposed to go?

The concept was as confusing as it was intangible. It felt like everyone was excited about this new world, but I was stuck trying to figure out how to get into it. Even when I asked how to use the internet to find information about how to get on the internet, the circular answers made me feel like I was running in place.

I wasn't alone in my confusion either. I distinctly remember watching Bill Gates on the David Letterman show, where Letterman was poking fun at Gates, trying to get him to explain what the internet actually was. Gates, the mastermind behind Microsoft, gave answers that were still abstract, and even Letterman seemed amused by how unclear it all was. It made me realize that even the biggest tech innovators struggled to explain this new digital frontier in simple terms. At that moment, I felt a bit of relief—if David Letterman and Bill Gates were having a hard time nailing down an explanation, then I wasn't too far off in my confusion!

Eventually, I did "get on the internet" and to be honest, my first experience was a bit underwhelming. There were no flashing lights or miraculous discoveries right off the bat. I remember thinking, "Is this it? Is this what everyone's been so hyped about?" It felt like the promise of the internet was always bigger than the reality in those early days. But, like anything in the digital world, it eventually caught up with itself. What seemed like endless potential slowly started to make sense as more people joined, websites improved, and the internet became the global powerhouse of information it is today.

But those early days? It was like stepping into a fog, knowing that something incredible was out there, but not quite sure how to reach it or what to expect once I did.

## The Value and Purpose of Networks and the Internet in God's Plan

At their core, networks and the internet are about connection—connecting people, ideas, and resources. They allow for collaboration, the sharing of knowledge, and the building of relationships across the globe. From a spiritual perspective, this mirrors God's plan for humanity: to be united, to share the message of Christ, and to support one another in love.

Ephesians 4:16 describes how the body of Christ grows through connection: "From him, the whole body joined and held together by every supporting ligament, grows and builds itself up in love, as each part does its work." Just as networks and the internet connect systems and enable them to function together, God calls us to be connected in fellowship and ministry, working together for His Kingdom.

The internet has brought incredible value to ministries, evangelism, and the sharing of the Gospel. Ministries can now reach people in the most remote parts of the world, spreading the message of Christ in places that may otherwise be inaccessible. The internet has made Matthew 28:19, the Great Commission to "go and make disciples of all nations," more achievable than ever before. Through online platforms, social media, and digital tools, the Gospel can be shared across the globe in seconds.

# The Distinction Between Networks and the Internet

While **networks** are limited to smaller, localized systems, the **internet** serves as the bridge that connects those individual networks on a global scale. Here's how they work together and yet remain distinct:

1. **Networks**: These are confined to specific locations (e.g., an office, home, or university). A network enables devices within that space to communicate and share resources. A local network can function without needing the internet, though it is often enhanced by connecting to the broader web.

2. **The Internet**: The internet is a vast, global network made up of smaller networks like the ones mentioned above. It relies on **TCP/IP protocols** to link different systems together, making it possible for a computer in the United States to access information stored on a server in Japan. The internet relies on the existence of networks, and networks can gain access to global resources through the internet.

Much like how the body of Christ has individual members that function independently but are united in purpose, networks function on their own but are most powerful when connected to the greater whole—just as believers are most effective when connected in unity through Christ.

## God's Master Plan for Connectivity

In the same way that God used the printing press during the Reformation to spread the Bible, He is using networks and the internet today to spread His message to every corner of the world. These technologies have made it possible for the Gospel to be shared in unprecedented ways, with millions of people accessing sermons, Scripture, and spiritual encouragement online.

Isaiah 55:11 reminds us, "So shall my word be that goes out from my mouth; it shall not return to me empty, but it shall accomplish that

which I purpose and shall succeed in the thing for which I sent it."
Through networks and the internet, God's Word is reaching people
who may have never heard the Gospel through traditional means. His
divine plan is unfolding in ways that the early developers of networks
and the internet could never have imagined.

## Conclusion: The Divine Purpose of Networks and the Internet

The development of networks and the internet is a powerful testament
to God's faithfulness and the ingenuity He has given to humanity.
These systems, though initially created for practical purposes, have
become tools for advancing the Kingdom of God, connecting
believers, and spreading the Gospel across the globe. Networks and
the internet work hand-in-hand, much like the body of Christ functions
as individual parts united in purpose.

God's creative power and His plan for connectivity are evident in the
history and ongoing development of these technologies. As believers,
we are called to recognize the divine potential of these tools and use
them to fulfill the Great Commission, knowing that through networks
and the internet, God is accomplishing His purposes in ways that reach
far beyond what we can imagine.

# Chapter 6

## Divine Innovation: How God Orchestrated the Rise of Software, Apps, and Cloud and Future Computing for His Greater Purpose

### The Rise of Software, Apps, and Cloud Computing: A Reflection of God's Creative Power

The development of **software** is one of the most profound milestones in the history of technology, and it stands as a testament to **God's creative power** and orchestration over human innovation. While the **hardware**—the physical components of a computer—creates the structure, the **software** provides the soul that brings it to life. From the very first lines of code to the complex apps and cloud systems we use today, **God's guiding hand** can be seen in the way software has evolved to meet the needs of humanity, reflecting His wisdom and creativity.

The story of software begins with the earliest computers, which were originally programmed using **machine code**—a system of binary (1s and 0s) that gave computers instructions directly. Early programmers had to input instructions in this cumbersome way, making programming an incredibly complex and time-consuming process. It wasn't until the creation of **assembly language**, which allowed for easier human interaction with machines, that the concept of **software** as we understand it today began to take shape.

One of the earliest triumphs in software history was the development of **FORTRAN (Formula Translation)** in the 1950s, a programming language that allowed scientists and engineers to write programs that could perform mathematical calculations far more easily. **Grace Hopper**, a pioneer in computer science, also developed **COBOL (Common Business-Oriented Language)**, which became the foundation for business software applications. Through individuals like Hopper, God used **gifts of wisdom and innovation** to make computers more accessible, and their potential more fully realized. As the Bible reminds us in **James 1:5**, *"If any of you lacks wisdom, you should ask God, who gives generously to all without finding fault, and it will be given to you."*

As the 1970s and 1980s progressed, personal computing began to take off. Early software companies like **Microsoft**, founded by **Bill Gates** and **Paul Allen**, and **Apple**, founded by **Steve Jobs** and **Steve Wozniak**, played pivotal roles in shaping the future of software. **Microsoft** developed the **MS-DOS** operating system in 1981, which laid the groundwork for their highly successful **Windows** operating system in 1985. Meanwhile, **Apple** launched the **Macintosh** in 1984, which introduced a **graphical user interface (GUI)**, making computers easier for the average person to use. These operating systems were significant breakthroughs, allowing people to interact with computers without needing to know complex programming languages. It was a **God-inspired leap** in usability, bringing the power of computing to the masses.

With the rise of these operating systems came the birth of **software applications**—or apps. Early software was mainly focused on tasks like **word processing, spreadsheets**, and **basic data management**, but as computing power grew, so did the scope of what software could accomplish. The development of applications like **Lotus 1-2-3** (an early spreadsheet program) and **WordStar** (an early word processor) made computing practical for businesses, but these were just the beginning.

The explosion of the **internet** in the 1990s opened the door for entirely new categories of software. Web browsers like **Netscape Navigator** and **Internet Explorer** allowed users to navigate the World Wide Web, while email applications like **Outlook** made communication instantaneous. These developments, though driven by human ambition and vision, were part of a **larger divine plan**, as they laid the groundwork for a world where information could be shared and accessed with unprecedented speed and efficiency. As **Proverbs 19:21** reminds us, *"Many are the plans in a person's heart, but it is the Lord's purpose that prevails."*

## Successes and Failures: God's Guidance Through It All

The journey of software development has not been without its **failures**, but these challenges have often paved the way for greater successes. One of the most famous failures in the software world was the **Windows Vista** operating system, released by Microsoft in 2007. Plagued by bugs, performance issues, and compatibility problems, Vista was widely regarded as a failure both by users and critics. However, Microsoft learned from this setback, and within two years, they released **Windows 7**, which became one of the most successful and beloved operating systems in history. This mirrors how God often allows us to **experience failures** so that we can grow, learn, and ultimately succeed in ways that glorify Him. **Proverbs 24:16** says, *"For though the righteous fall seven times, they rise again."* Even in the world of technology, God's lessons on perseverance and redemption apply.

Similarly, **Apple** experienced its own failures with products like the **Apple Newton**, an early attempt at a personal digital assistant (PDA), which failed to capture the market. Yet, from these failures came tremendous success with devices like the **iPhone** and **iPad**, which revolutionized mobile computing. God's hand can be seen in how these companies have rebounded from their challenges, creating technologies that have changed the way we live, work, and communicate.

## Mastering Intuitive Software: A Journey Through User Experience and Innovation

My journey with software has been, like many others, multifaceted and ever-evolving. I don't really remember when I first became aware of how software worked. It feels like my life has always involved managing, updating, and learning about software, almost as if it's a constant companion in my day-to-day routine.

Software defines our experience with computers. Every time we sit in front of a screen, it's the software we're interacting with. Without it, a computer is just a piece of hardware with no real purpose. If someone unfamiliar with computers had to describe one, they'd likely focus on the software they know rather than the hardware itself. For most people, the programs they use are what they associate with their computers—the apps, the interfaces, and the tools that make their work or entertainment possible.

Because of this, our relationship with computers is personal and shaped by the software we use. In my day-to-day work, I own and run a few different companies, but the one I spend the most time on is a cybersecurity app. We constantly work on understanding the user experience and making our software more intuitive so that users don't have to struggle to figure it out. It's incredibly rewarding when we receive feedback from users who are enjoying their experience with our newly designed software. Knowing that we've made their lives easier is one of the best parts of what we do.

What makes software truly great is its ability to anticipate what we're thinking and predict our next move, often before we even realize what we're going to do. The more intuitive the software is, the more seamlessly it integrates into our work or play. But when software falls short of this, frustration sets in—especially when I've spent time learning someone's program, only for them to suddenly change it in the name of improvement. I always think, "You should have made things better before I learned it—now is not the time to switch things up!" I know that's not realistic, but it's one of the more frustrating aspects of software.

It's also exasperating when I expect a feature to be there—something I've grown accustomed to in other programs only to find that it's missing. I imagine it should be there because other software has it in that spot, so why doesn't this one? Fortunately, as software evolves, I've noticed that many programs start to mimic each other, leading to more standardized interfaces and experiences. This growing universality makes things smoother as everything becomes more aligned.

Still, without software, most of the day-to-day tasks we rely on computers for would be worthless. It's the programs themselves that breathe life into these machines. I'm excited to see how software continues to advance, especially as technology becomes more powerful. The future will likely bring even more intuitive, intelligent software that makes working with computers feel almost effortless.

## Software's Impact on Humanity and God's Orchestration

Software has had an undeniable impact on **every aspect of modern life**. Applications have transformed industries like **banking**, **healthcare**, **education**, and **entertainment**. What once took days or weeks to accomplish can now be done in seconds through **digital apps**. Consider how **banking apps** allow people to transfer funds across the globe with a click or how **healthcare software** can now analyze patient data to deliver faster and more accurate diagnoses. Even in education, apps like **Khan Academy** and **Duolingo** have democratized learning, allowing people around the world to access knowledge that was once only available to a select few.

Behind all of these advancements is **God's orchestration**. Through software, God has provided humanity with tools that, when used wisely, can **benefit the world** and improve lives. **Colossians 3:17** reminds us, *"And whatever you do, in word or deed, do everything in the name of the Lord Jesus, giving thanks to God the Father through Him."* Software is no different—it is a tool that can be used to **glorify God**, connect His people, and fulfill His purposes.

# The Emergence of Cloud Computing: A New Era of Software and God's Guidance

One of the most **transformative advancements** in software and technology over the past two decades has been the rise of **cloud computing**. It represents a new era in the way data is stored, managed, and accessed, marking a shift from the traditional model of localized computing to a **global, interconnected network**. This development has not only revolutionized the tech industry but has had far-reaching effects on business, education, healthcare, and even personal lives. As with all technological advancements, **God's hand** can be seen orchestrating the rise of cloud computing, providing humanity with tools to foster greater **collaboration, efficiency, and connection** in ways that were previously unimaginable.

## Traditional Computing vs. Cloud Computing

To understand the **impact of cloud computing**, it's essential to compare it with the traditional computing model first. In traditional computing, both software and data are stored **locally** on a user's computer or an on-site server. This meant that to access specific files or applications. Users needed to be physically present at their computer or connected to their local network. While this model served well in the early days of computing, it posed several limitations, such as the risk of data loss from hardware failure, limited storage capacity, and the challenge of collaboration when multiple users needed to work on the same files.

The emergence of **cloud computing** in the early 2000s offered a groundbreaking solution. **Cloud computing** stores your data and software on remote servers - what we call 'the cloud.' You can access everything over the internet from any device. This system works like a power grid for software, letting you tap into powerful computers anywhere in the world. God's design for community and connection is reflected in how cloud computing brings people and resources together.. This means that users are no longer tethered to a specific machine or location. Instead, they can access their data and software **anywhere, anytime,** as long as they have an internet connection. This fundamental shift in computing has opened incredible opportunities for **collaboration, scalability**, and **innovation**.

Major cloud platforms like **Amazon Web Services (AWS)**, **Google Cloud**, and **Microsoft Azure** were developed to meet the growing demand for cloud computing. These platforms offer a range of cloud-based services, from **data storage** and **virtual computing** to **machine learning** and **AI tools**, allowing businesses and individuals to store, analyze, and manage data on a massive scale. By eliminating the need for extensive on-site infrastructure, cloud computing has made **powerful technology accessible** to even the smallest businesses and individual users.

## Successes of Cloud Computing

The benefits of cloud computing are vast, and its **success** has been evident in numerous industries:

1. **Scalability**: One of the most significant advantages of cloud computing is its **scalability**. Businesses no longer need to invest in costly hardware to expand their operations. Instead, they can simply increase their cloud storage or processing power as needed, allowing them to grow or shrink their IT infrastructure depending on demand. This has been especially beneficial for startups and small businesses that can now access enterprise-level technology without significant upfront costs.

2. **Collaboration**: Cloud computing has revolutionized the way teams work together. For instance, tools like **Google Docs**

allow multiple users to collaborate on a single document in real time, no matter where they are in the world. This level of collaboration has dramatically increased productivity and efficiency, allowing teams to work together on projects from different time zones and devices. **Dropbox** and **OneDrive** offer seamless file storage and sharing across devices, making it easier than ever to share information and work together on documents.

3. **Cost Efficiency**: Cloud computing has reduced the need for businesses to maintain large data centers and on-site servers. Instead of purchasing and maintaining expensive hardware, companies can **pay for cloud services on a subscription basis**, meaning they only pay for the resources they use. This has saved businesses millions of dollars in infrastructure and maintenance costs.

4. **Data Backup and Recovery**: One of the greatest risks of traditional computing was **data loss** due to hardware failure or disaster. Cloud computing mitigates this risk by automatically backing up data to remote servers, ensuring that data is protected and can be recovered in the event of an emergency. This added layer of security has been a **lifesaver** for many businesses and individuals who might otherwise have lost valuable information.

5. **Innovation**: The flexibility and accessibility of cloud computing have enabled **rapid innovation** in fields like **AI**, **machine learning**, and **big data analysis**. Companies can now run complex simulations, analyze massive datasets, and implement new technologies without the need for expensive hardware or extensive IT support. This has accelerated the pace of technological development across multiple sectors, from **healthcare** to **finance**.

## Failures and Risks of Cloud Computing

However, as with any major advancement, **cloud computing** has also faced its share of challenges and **failures**:

1. **Security Concerns**: One of the primary concerns with cloud computing is data **security**. While cloud providers invest heavily in security measures, the centralized nature of the cloud means that if a breach occurs, it could potentially compromise **vast amounts of data** across multiple users or businesses. High-profile data breaches involving cloud services have caused many to question the security and privacy of cloud storage.

2. **Downtime**: Even the largest and most reliable cloud providers are not immune to **downtime**. When a cloud platform experiences technical issues or outages, it can disrupt businesses that rely on these services for day-to-day operations. While this is relatively rare, downtime can result in significant financial losses for companies that depend on constant access to their data and applications.

3. **Vendor Lock-in**: Another potential risk of cloud computing is **vendor lock-in**, where a business becomes so dependent on a specific cloud provider's services that switching to a competitor becomes costly or difficult. This can limit flexibility and stifle competition in the long term.

4. **Privacy Issues**: The rise of cloud computing has also sparked debates about **privacy** and who really controls the data stored on cloud servers. Users often must trust that their cloud provider will protect their personal information and not misuse or share it with third parties. This concern has been heightened by incidents where cloud providers have shared user data with governments or private entities without explicit consent.

## How Cloud Computing Works

To explain **cloud computing** in simple terms, imagine that instead of storing files on your computer's hard drive, you store them in a **giant digital filing cabinet** located somewhere far away. You can access this cabinet from any computer, smartphone, or tablet, as long as you're connected to the internet. The key difference is that this cabinet (the cloud) is managed by companies like **AWS**, **Google**, or **Microsoft**, who ensure that the files are always available, secure, and backed up.

Cloud services are typically delivered in three forms:

1.  **Infrastructure as a Service (IaaS)**: This provides virtualized computing resources over the internet, like **virtual machines** or **servers**, which businesses can use to run their own software and store data. IaaS allows businesses to **rent computing power** and storage space rather than investing in physical hardware.
2.  **Platform as a Service (PaaS)**: This offers a platform that allows developers to build, test, and deploy software applications without managing the underlying infrastructure. Services like **Google App Engine** and **AWS Elastic Beanstalk** are examples of PaaS, providing environments where developers can focus solely on writing code without worrying about hardware.
3.  **Software as a Service (SaaS)**: This is the most familiar form of cloud computing for everyday users. SaaS delivers fully functional software applications over the internet, such as **Google Docs**, **Salesforce**, or **Microsoft 365**. Users access these applications via a web browser without installing or maintaining the software on their devices.

## Embracing the Cloud: My Journey to a Global, Connected, and Efficient Business

The advancement of software into the cloud has truly created a new world, one I never imagined we'd be operating in a decade ago. At first, I was hesitant. The idea of storing all my data somewhere beyond my control seemed risky, even reckless. Why would I put all my company's sensitive information on something that wasn't physically in my office or on my own computer? It felt too uncertain, like giving up control over my own operations.

But, as with many emerging technologies, my skepticism began to wane as cloud computing advanced. As security technology improved, so did my trust in the system. It wasn't just an interesting concept anymore—it became a practical and secure solution for modern business. Over time, I grew more comfortable with the idea, realizing the immense potential of having everything accessible beyond the walls of my office.

Today, nearly all of our business operations are cloud-based. This shift has allowed our employees to collaborate seamlessly from anywhere in the world. We have team members in Portugal, Mongolia, the Philippines, and across the United States, all working together on the same software and accessing the same information in real-time. The ability for us to function globally without barriers is incredible. Just 10 years ago, I couldn't have imagined being this connected working across multiple time zones as if we were all sitting in the same office.

One of the most significant changes cloud computing has brought is the need—or lack thereof—for physical offices. While I still appreciate the value of having a physical space where people can meet, brainstorm, and solve problems together, cloud computing has drastically reduced the necessity of being tied to a specific location. Now, we can operate as a truly global team, with contributions from people who, due to geographic barriers, would have never been part of our company's innovation and growth before.

Take our cybersecurity app, for example. It's now being used in over 40 countries, offering protection for devices anywhere in the world. This global reach is a direct result of the cloud-based infrastructure we've adopted. The cloud makes it all possible, allowing us to deliver our service globally with consistent quality and security. It's one of the most powerful aspects of cloud computing: the ability to scale, protect, and maintain our product across the world, regardless of where our users are located.

On a personal level, cloud computing has made my life more efficient as well. I manage multiple businesses, which means I have several offices in which to work. A few years ago, I got tired of carrying a computer from one office to another every day, so I set up dedicated computers in each of my offices, all of them completely synchronized via the cloud. If I respond to an email in one office, everything is updated and ready when I sit down at the next. If I access a document at one location, I can pull it up instantly at my next meeting in a different office. This seamless integration across my offices has been a game-changer, allowing me to focus more on the work at hand instead of the logistics of moving between locations.

Even in my car, I have a computer that accesses the cloud, but it's set up with minimal information, just enough to connect me to everything I need. That's the beauty of cloud computing—my data isn't tied to a single device. It's accessible anywhere, anytime, on any device I choose, making my day-to-day operations more streamlined and efficient.

Cloud computing will only continue to make our world more connected and efficient. It's already revolutionized how we work, communicate, and innovate, and I'm excited to see where it takes us next. The ability to work globally, securely, and without boundaries is transforming business as we know it.

## The Spiritual Connection: God's Providential Hand

The rise of cloud computing is not just a technological achievement but also a reflection of **God's providence**. This system of interconnected data and collaboration mirrors the **unity and cooperation** that God desires for His people. Just as cloud computing allows for the **sharing of resources** and **instant communication**, God calls us to **share our spiritual gifts** and work together for the **common good**.

As believers, we can see the **hand of God** in the development of cloud computing, which enables people from different parts of the world to come together in ways that were once impossible. Cloud computing provides **greater access** to information and tools, mirroring how **God**

**freely offers His wisdom and guidance** to all who seek Him. **James 1:5** reminds us, *"If any of you lacks wisdom, you should ask God, who gives generously to all without finding fault, and it will be given to you."*

While cloud computing, like any technology, has its risks and challenges, we must remember that **God is sovereign** over all things, including the digital world. Just as He orchestrated the rise of computing and software, He continues to guide the advancement of cloud technologies for the **benefit of His people** and the **fulfillment of His purposes**.

As we navigate the benefits and risks of cloud computing, we are reminded of the need for **wisdom** and **discernment** in how we use these tools. Ultimately, cloud computing has the potential to enhance our ability to work together, share knowledge, and connect with one another in ways that reflect **God's desire for unity and collaboration**. It is up to us to use this technology wisely, ensuring that it is a tool for good, a means of **glorifying God**, and a resource for **serving others**.

# AI (Artificial Intelligence): A Deep Dive into Its Origins, Functionality, and God's Role in Its Development

**Artificial Intelligence (AI)** is a branch of computer science focused on creating machines and software capable of performing tasks that would normally require **human intelligence**. These tasks include recognizing patterns, making decisions, understanding languages, solving problems, and even mimicking human behavior. AI has evolved into one of the most transformative technologies of our time, affecting industries as diverse as healthcare, finance, education, transportation, and entertainment. But how does AI work, and what is its history? Moreover, where is it going, and how can we understand **God's role** in the development of this powerful technology?

# What is AI?

At its core, **artificial intelligence** is about creating systems that can **learn** and **adapt** to new information, allowing them to perform tasks that would normally require human intelligence. There are two main types of AI:

1. **Narrow AI**: This is the most common form of AI in use today. Narrow AI is designed to perform specific tasks, such as recognizing faces in photos, recommending movies, or driving a car. It does not possess general intelligence or consciousness but is extremely effective at the task for which it has been trained.
2. **General AI**: This is the hypothetical form of AI that many researchers are working toward. General AI would be capable of performing **any intellectual task** that a human can do. It would not be limited to a specific domain but could learn and adapt across a wide range of fields, like how human intelligence works.

Within these categories, AI systems rely on several key technologies:

- **Machine Learning (ML)**: Machine learning is a subset of AI that involves teaching machines to learn from data. Instead of being explicitly programmed to perform a task, the machine learns from examples and adjusts its performance based on patterns in the data.
- **Neural Networks**: Modeled after the human brain, neural networks consist of layers of interconnected nodes (or neurons) that process data. Neural networks are used in many modern AI applications, particularly in **deep learning**, where these networks can have many layers (hence the term "deep").
- **Natural Language Processing (NLP)**: NLP enables AI systems to understand, interpret, and generate human language. This is the technology behind **voice assistants** like **Siri** and **Alexa**, as well as translation services and chatbots.

- **Computer Vision**: This allows AI to interpret visual data from the world, such as recognizing faces, objects, or scenes in images and videos.
- **Robotics**: AI is also applied in robotics, where it gives machines the ability to perform tasks autonomously, such as self-driving cars, drones, or industrial robots.

## How Does AI Work?

AI systems are built on **algorithms**, which are step-by-step procedures or formulas for solving problems. These algorithms are trained using **large datasets**. For instance, if you want an AI to recognize cats in photos, you will feed it thousands or millions of pictures of cats. The AI learns from these examples, adjusting its internal parameters until it can correctly identify a cat when it sees one.

This process of **learning from data** is known as **supervised learning**, where the machine learns from labeled data (e.g., pictures that have been labeled "cat" or "not cat"). Over time, the AI system improves its accuracy, and with enough data and computing power, it can perform the task as well as or better than a human.

AI also uses **unsupervised learning**, where the machine is given data without explicit labels and must find patterns on its own, and **reinforcement learning**, where an AI learns by trial and error, receiving rewards for correct actions and penalties for incorrect ones.

## The History of AI

The idea of creating machines that could think and reason like humans has existed for centuries, even appearing in ancient mythology. However, AI as a scientific field began in the **mid-20th century**.

1. **Early Foundations (1940s-1950s)**: The conceptual groundwork for AI was laid by early computer scientists like **Alan Turing**, who, in his 1950 paper *"Computing Machinery and Intelligence"*, asked the famous question, *"Can machines*

*think?"* He proposed the **Turing Test**, a method for determining whether a machine could exhibit intelligent behavior indistinguishable from a human. Turing's ideas were pivotal in shaping the future of AI.

2. **The Birth of AI (1956)**: AI was officially born as a field of study during the **Dartmouth Conference** in 1956, organized by **John McCarthy, Marvin Minsky, Claude Shannon**, and **Nathaniel Rochester**. These researchers proposed that human intelligence could be precisely described and that a machine could be built to simulate it.

3. **The Early AI Boom (1950s-1970s)**: Early AI research focused on developing algorithms that could solve problems and play games like chess. The 1960s saw the development of **Expert Systems**, designed to mimic human decision-making in specific fields. However, these early systems were limited by the technology of the time, particularly the lack of powerful computers.

4. **AI Winters (1970s-1990s)**: AI experienced several periods of disillusionment known as **AI winters**, during which funding and interest in AI research dwindled. Many early promises of AI—such as achieving human-like general intelligence—proved far more difficult to achieve than initially thought.

5. **The AI Renaissance (1990s-present)**: In the late 1990s and early 2000s, AI research was reinvigorated by advances in **computing power**, **data availability**, and **machine learning algorithms**. Breakthroughs in **neural networks** and **deep learning** led to rapid improvements in AI's ability to perform complex tasks, such as speech recognition, image classification, and game-playing. Notably, **IBM's Deep Blue** defeated world chess champion **Garry Kasparov** in 1997, and in 2016, **Google DeepMind's AlphaGo** defeated the world champion in **Go**, a game far more complex than chess.

Today, AI powers a wide range of applications, from self-driving cars and smart home assistants to healthcare diagnostics and financial forecasting.

# How Was God Involved in the Development of AI?

As believers, we recognize that **God is sovereign** over all creation, including the development of technology. From the early pioneers like **Alan Turing** to modern AI researchers, God has **endowed humanity** with the wisdom and creativity to pursue such groundbreaking work. The skills, knowledge, and innovations behind AI come from God's wisdom. As **James 1:17** tells us, *"Every good and perfect gift is from above, coming down from the Father of the heavenly lights."* The skills, knowledge, and innovations behind AI are no exception.

While AI often seems like a human achievement, it is important to acknowledge the **divine inspiration** that allows such technological advancements. Just as God gifted individuals throughout history with the insight to build things like the **steam engine**, the **printing press**, and the **telephone**, He has provided the intellect and tools to develop AI. **Proverbs 2:6** reminds us, *"For the Lord gives wisdom; from his mouth comes knowledge and understanding."* Every algorithm, every line of code, and every neural network was built on the foundation of **God-given wisdom**.

AI can also be seen as a reflection of God's **creative nature**. We, made in **God's image** (Genesis 1:27), have been given the ability to **create** and **innovate**, just as God created the world. AI represents one of the many ways in which humans are fulfilling their **mandate to cultivate** and **steward** the earth (Genesis 1:28), using the tools God has provided to improve lives and solve complex problems.

## Successes and Failures in AI

The journey of AI development has been marked by both **remarkable successes** and **disappointing failures**, and in these, we can see how God has used both to further human knowledge and wisdom.

**Successes:**

1. **Healthcare**: AI has made tremendous advancements in **healthcare**. Algorithms are now able to analyze medical images and detect diseases like cancer with greater accuracy than human doctors in some cases. AI is also being used to develop new drugs and create personalized treatment plans. The ability to **save lives** and improve healthcare access through AI is a **blessing** that reflects God's care for humanity.
2. **Natural Language Processing**: Tools like **Google Translate**, **Siri**, and **Alexa** have made it easier for people to communicate across languages and access information instantly. AI's ability to understand and generate human language has revolutionized how we interact with machines, helping people with disabilities, improving customer service, and facilitating cross-cultural dialogue.
3. **Autonomous Vehicles**: Self-driving cars, powered by AI, have the potential to significantly reduce **traffic accidents** and make transportation more efficient. The development of AI in transportation is a reflection of God's desire for us to create systems that benefit society and improve safety.

**Failures:**

1. **Ethical Concerns**: AI has raised serious **ethical concerns**, particularly in areas like **surveillance**, **bias**, and **autonomous weapons**. AI systems are only as good as the data they are trained on, and biased or incomplete data can result in unfair or harmful outcomes, especially in areas like **criminal justice** or **hiring practices**. **God's Word** calls us to pursue **justice and fairness** (Micah 6:8), and as AI becomes more integrated into our society, we must ensure that it is used for **good** rather than perpetuating **injustice**.
2. **Job Displacement**: One of the unintended consequences of AI is its potential to replace human workers in industries ranging from **manufacturing** to **customer service**. While AI can increase productivity, it also raises concerns about **economic inequality** and job loss. As we navigate these changes, we must remember God's call to care for the

vulnerable (Matthew 25:35-40) and ensure that technological advancements do not leave people behind.

## Navigating the Promise and Perils of AI: A Faith-Based Approach to Embracing Technology

AI is a fascinating and powerful technology, much like the other technological advances that have shaped our world. But as with any new technology, it can feel a little scary at first, especially if you're someone who naturally asks, "What can go wrong?" I've had that same feeling with each new leap—whether it was cloud computing, the internet, or even the very first computers. It's always been a process of trying to figure out both the potential and the risks. With AI, I feel the same combination of excitement for what it could do and nervousness about the vulnerabilities it may open.

AI brings incredible possibilities. Its ability to analyze vast amounts of data, automate tasks, and even predict outcomes could revolutionize countless industries—healthcare, education, business, and beyond. Imagine an AI system that can help diagnose diseases faster than a human doctor, offering quicker treatment and better outcomes for patients. Or think about how AI could enhance educational tools, customizing learning experiences for students all over the world and making sure each one has the support they need to thrive. These are the kinds of applications that make AI exciting.

But with that excitement comes the reality of risk. AI is a tool, and like any tool, it can be used for good or for harm. Just as I learned with cloud computing and cybersecurity, where there's technology, there's also the potential for misuse. The enemy can use the very same advances to create chaos, confusion, or outright harm. We've seen this pattern time and time again—whether it's hacking into systems, spreading disinformation, or invading privacy—bad actors will always try to exploit new technologies.

That's why, as believers, it's crucial for us to learn about AI, not just to understand its capabilities, but to find ways to use it to advance

God's greater plan while protecting ourselves from inevitable attacks. It's like navigating the internet or securing cloud-based systems. The more we know, the better equipped we are to use these tools for good while defending against the bad.

For instance, AI could be used to help spread the gospel more effectively, whether through personalized outreach or creating tools that help people engage with Scripture in new and meaningful ways. Ministries could benefit from AI-driven analytics, helping them understand where the greatest needs are and how to address them. Even day-to-day tasks like managing data or communications could be enhanced by AI, freeing up more time for people to focus on the mission at hand.

At the same time, we need to stay vigilant. AI's power to mimic human behavior could lead to serious threats, like deep fakes or AI-driven fraud. The technology can also be biased, reflecting the flaws of its creators, and if unchecked, it could lead to unintended consequences that might harm individuals or communities. This is why we must approach AI with wisdom and discernment, seeking to understand how to protect against these vulnerabilities.

There are practical steps we can take to protect ourselves while embracing AI. Staying informed about cybersecurity practices is essential ensuring that the data AI systems have access to is secure and that those using AI tools are trained to recognize potential threats. Implementing robust oversight and ethics into AI development is equally important, so we can avoid the pitfalls of misuse and bias.

Ultimately, just as we've navigated cloud computing, the internet, and software, we'll need to navigate AI with both excitement and caution. By embracing its potential and learning to protect ourselves from its risks, we can use AI not just for personal or business success, but as a tool to further God's kingdom in this digital age. With careful thought, responsible use, and faith, we can turn this powerful technology into a force for good, pushing back against the enemy's attempts to use it for harm. It's about staying one step ahead, learning and growing, and always keeping our eyes on the ultimate goal.

# Where is AI Going?

Looking to the future, **AI's capabilities** will continue to grow. AI will likely play an increasingly significant role in **medicine, education, transportation**, and even **art**. The development of **General AI**— machines capable of reasoning and learning at human-like levels— remains a long-term goal, though it is still far from being realized.

The key question for the future of AI is not just what it can do, but how we will use it. **God's sovereignty** extends to all things, including technology. As we move into an AI-powered future, we must seek God's wisdom and guidance to ensure that AI is used in ways that glorify Him and serve humanity. **Colossians 3:17** reminds us, *"And whatever you do, whether in word or deed, do it all in the name of the Lord Jesus, giving thanks to God the Father through him."* This includes our work with AI, ensuring that it is used for **good**, uplifting society and protecting human dignity.

# AI as a Reflection of God's Wisdom

In the story of **AI's development**, we can see God's fingerprints in the wisdom, creativity, and progress that has shaped this powerful technology. While AI presents both incredible opportunities and significant challenges, we are called to **steward** this technology wisely, recognizing that God is the ultimate source of all knowledge and innovation. By seeking His guidance, we can ensure that AI serves as a tool for **good**, advancing **human flourishing** and reflecting the **creative power of God**.

# The History of Apps: Origins, Development, and Impact

## The Birth of Applications: From the Early Days to Modern Innovations

Applications, commonly known as **apps**, are software programs designed to perform specific tasks for users. They have become an integral part of modern life, transforming the way we work, communicate, entertain, and learn. The development of apps is a story of human ingenuity that has roots in the earliest days of **computing**, evolving through decades of innovation into the digital age we know today.

But behind all this innovation, there is a higher orchestration. God, the ultimate source of wisdom and creativity, has been working through human minds and hands, guiding the development of applications to fulfill His greater purposes—empowering people, improving lives, and providing new ways to connect and share His truth.

### Early Beginnings: The First "Applications"

The concept of software applications can be traced back to the origins of modern computing in the **1940s and 1950s**. Early computers, such as the **ENIAC** (Electronic Numerical Integrator and Computer) developed in 1945, were complex machines that performed specific calculations for military and scientific purposes. These early machines were operated through punch cards and wiring changes, requiring significant manual input to perform tasks.

The first true "application" was a piece of software written to perform tasks such as solving mathematical problems or organizing data more efficiently. One of the earliest breakthroughs came in 1957 with the creation of **FORTRAN** (Formula Translation), the first high-level programming language designed for scientific and engineering applications. **Grace Hopper**, an early pioneer in computer science, also developed **COBOL** (Common Business-Oriented Language) in 1959, which became widely used in business and government applications for decades.

These early applications were mostly focused on **mathematical computation**, data processing, and administrative functions, often running on **mainframe computers** used by large organizations. The concept of personal computing and user-friendly applications was still far off in the future.

# The Personal Computer Era: Democratizing Software

The development of the **personal computer (PC)** in the 1970s and 1980s by companies like **Apple** and **Microsoft** opened the door for the rise of software applications designed for individual users. **Microsoft**, founded by **Bill Gates** and **Paul Allen**, created the **MS-DOS** operating system in 1981, which allowed users to interact with computers using typed commands. However, it was the development of **graphical user interfaces (GUIs)**, such as **Apple's Macintosh** in 1984 and **Microsoft Windows** in 1985, that made personal computers more accessible to the general public.

The rise of personal computers and user-friendly operating systems (as we explored in Chapter 5) opened the door for **consumer-focused applications,** such as word processors, spreadsheets, and databases. This democratization of technology reflects God's desire for His gifts to be accessible to all His children.. **WordPerfect**, **Lotus 1-2-3**, and **Microsoft Excel** became essential tools for business, empowering people to perform complex tasks more efficiently than ever before. With the advent of user-friendly operating systems, applications became a fundamental part of everyday computing.

God's hand was at work even in these developments. The democratization of technology made it possible for individuals from all walks of life to access tools that could enhance their productivity, creativity, and connection with others. This reflects God's desire for

**human flourishing** and the empowerment of His people to fulfill their potential. As **Proverbs 8:12** reminds us: "I, wisdom, dwell with prudence, and I find knowledge and discretion."

## The Rise of the Internet and Web-Based Applications

The **1990s** saw the explosive growth of the **internet**, a revolutionary development that would redefine the purpose and functionality of applications. The introduction of the **World Wide Web** in 1991 by **Tim Berners-Lee** enabled people to access information from across the globe, sparking a wave of innovation in web-based applications.

**Web browsers** like **Netscape Navigator** and **Internet Explorer** became the first widely used applications for navigating the web, allowing people to access websites, share information, and connect with others online. The internet also gave rise to new types of applications, including **email clients** like **Outlook** and **Eudora**, as well as **e-commerce platforms** like **Amazon** and **eBay**. These apps began transforming industries, from retail to communications, enabling people to engage in **online shopping**, **banking**, and **business**.

Through these web-based applications, God was opening new avenues for **communication** and **collaboration**. The internet became a tool for spreading knowledge, building communities, and even sharing the **Gospel** across borders and cultures. Ministries and churches began to recognize the potential of the web to reach people in remote areas, bringing the **Word of God** to those who might never have encountered it otherwise (Matthew 28:19-20).

## Mobile Revolution: The App Store and the Rise of Mobile Applications

The most significant shift in the history of applications came with the advent of **smartphones** and **mobile apps**. In 2007, **Apple** launched the **iPhone**, a device that combined a phone, an iPod, and a mobile internet communicator. A year later, **Apple's App Store** was launched, offering a centralized platform where users could download a wide range of applications, from productivity tools to entertainment apps. This revolutionized the software industry, making applications readily available to anyone with a smartphone.

The success of the **App Store** inspired other companies like **Google** to launch their own app marketplaces, such as **Google Play** for Android devices. Today, millions of apps are available to perform almost any function imaginable—whether it's **social media** (Facebook, Instagram), **productivity** (Slack, Google Docs), **entertainment** (Spotify, Netflix), or **navigation** (Google Maps, Waze).

Through mobile apps, **God's glory** shines in new ways. Mobile technology has enabled ministries to develop Bible apps, such as the **YouVersion Bible App**, which has been downloaded by hundreds of millions of people worldwide. People can now carry the **Word of God** in their pockets, reading Scripture and engaging in devotional plans anytime and anywhere. Apps have also allowed for the **live streaming** of church services, making worship accessible to people who cannot physically attend. **Romans 10:17** says, "So faith comes from hearing, and hearing through the word of Christ," and through mobile technology, this can happen on a **global scale**.

## Cloud Computing and the Future of Apps

The next major leap in application development came with the rise of **cloud computing**. Instead of installing software on individual computers, cloud computing enables users to access applications through the internet. Platforms like **Google Drive**, **Dropbox**, and **Microsoft Office 365** allow for seamless collaboration, file sharing, and real-time editing across devices and locations.

The power of cloud-based applications lies in their ability to **scale** and **integrate** across large networks. This has revolutionized industries such as **healthcare**, **education**, and **business**, allowing for **remote work**, **telemedicine**, and **global collaboration**. Applications like **Zoom** and **Slack** became essential tools for staying connected, especially during the global pandemic, when physical gatherings were restricted.

God's **providential hand** is evident in cloud technology. Through it, believers are able to remain connected, even when circumstances prevent physical community. The global Church has been able to meet virtually, pray together, and encourage one another through apps that foster unity. **Ephesians 4:12** speaks of equipping the saints "for the work of ministry, for building up the body of Christ," and through technology, the body of Christ can remain connected across vast distances.

## The Role of Artificial Intelligence and Machine Learning in Apps

In recent years, the integration of **artificial intelligence (AI)** and **machine learning** into applications has taken them to a new level. **AI-powered apps** can now analyze data, predict user behavior, and offer personalized experiences. **Virtual assistants** like **Siri**, **Alexa**, and **Google Assistant** use AI to interact with users, manage tasks, and provide information.

AI's potential to **solve complex problems**, automate tasks, and improve efficiency reflects God's design for **order** and **wisdom** in creation (1 Corinthians 14:33). While AI can be used for both good and evil, it is ultimately a tool that can be harnessed for God's purposes. Ministries are now exploring AI-powered apps for **spiritual counseling**, **prayer support**, and **Bible study assistance**.

## Future of Apps: Technology for God's Glory

The future of applications will likely be driven by advancements in **5G technology**, **virtual reality (VR)**, **augmented reality (AR)**, and **blockchain**. These innovations will create new opportunities for believers to engage with the world, foster community, and spread the Gospel in ways we have yet to imagine.

As technology advances, **God's sovereignty** over human creativity continues to be revealed. While the **enemy** may seek to use technology for evil, **God will redeem it** for His glory. Apps have the potential to transform how we experience **worship**, **ministry**, and **fellowship** in the digital age. Whether through VR church services, AI-driven Bible study apps, or blockchain-based charity platforms, God is guiding His people to use technology for **good**.

**Colossians 3:17** reminds us, "And whatever you do, in word or deed, do everything in the name of the Lord Jesus, giving thanks to God the Father through him." This applies to the world of applications as well. When used with purpose and integrity, apps can serve as powerful tools to glorify God, connect believers, and advance His kingdom.

## Embracing the App Revolution: From Confusion to Integration and the Future of AI-Powered Solutions

It took me quite a while to fully understand what apps were. At first, I thought of them as just small, specific pieces of software designed to do certain things. But, as with most technology, it always takes me a bit to wrap my head around the concept. When apps first became popular, I didn't quite grasp that they could come in so many forms and serve such varied purposes. I assumed the early apps were named after the particular software they provided, not realizing they were a type of software altogether. It seems silly looking back, but that's often how communication works—you're told something new, and then you must figure out what it means based on what you already know.

Once I finally understood what apps were, I realized I needed to embrace a new kind of phone to access the "app world." That was a big shift for me, as I'd been accustomed to more traditional ways of using technology. But, as with most things, I adapted step by step, and now apps are an essential part of my daily life. It's amazing how much my world has changed because of them.

Today, apps are central to how I operate, both personally and professionally. We've even developed our own apps as part of my work. Now, whenever I encounter an issue or need a solution, my first instinct is to check the app store and see if someone has already created an app to solve it. It's become second nature. Whether it's managing security cameras, keeping track of my calendar, or checking the weather in various locations where we work, I rely on apps to access most of the things I need.

Over time, I've developed a rather elaborate system to organize all the apps I use. With so many apps designed for different tasks, from work to personal life, it's easy for things to get disorganized. But with my system, everything is streamlined, allowing me to quickly find and use the apps that keep my world running smoothly.

What I find most fascinating is thinking about the future of apps, especially as AI begins to play a bigger role in their development. AI has the potential to make apps even more efficient, enhancing their capabilities and tailoring them to individual needs in ways we've only begun to imagine. Whether it's apps that anticipate your next move, automate more complex tasks, or learn from your behavior to offer personalized suggestions, AI-powered apps are likely to revolutionize the way we use this technology.

Apps have already transformed how we manage our lives, and it's exciting to think about where things will go from here. The combination of artificial intelligence and app development could lead to solutions we haven't even dreamed of yet, making our lives more connected, efficient, and ultimately easier to navigate in this fast-paced world.

# Conclusion: God's Hand in the History and Future of Apps

From the early days of computing to the rise of mobile and cloud-based applications, **God's wisdom** has been at the center of technological innovation. Applications have revolutionized the way we live, work, and communicate, making the world more connected and accessible than ever before. In all of this, **God's glory** is reflected in the creativity, collaboration, and empowerment that apps bring to our lives. As we move forward, believers are called to **use technology responsibly** and in ways that **align with God's will**, always seeking to glorify Him in all things.

# Supercomputers: What Are They, How Do They Work, and Their Role in the Future

**Supercomputers** are the most powerful computational machines on the planet, capable of performing **trillions** of calculations per second, and processing massive amounts of data in record time. While a typical computer may be sufficient for everyday tasks like web browsing or word processing, **supercomputers** are used for highly complex computations in fields like **climate science**, **molecular modeling**, **cryptography**, **nuclear research**, and, more recently, **artificial intelligence (AI)**. These machines represent the pinnacle of computational power and are essential for solving problems that would be practically impossible to tackle with ordinary computers.

## What is a Supercomputer?

A **supercomputer** is a high-performance computing (HPC) machine specifically designed to solve extremely complex problems by processing and analyzing vast datasets at incredible speeds. The core difference between a supercomputer and a regular desktop or laptop computer is its **processing power** and the way it is built.

Supercomputers achieve their incredible performance by using **parallel processing**, a technique that allows thousands or even millions of processors to work together on a single problem at the same time. Traditional computers typically process tasks in a **sequential** manner—one task after another—while supercomputers split tasks into smaller parts that are distributed among many processors to be solved simultaneously. This results in **exponential increases in speed**.

## How Do Supercomputers Work?

Supercomputers are built with **thousands of individual processors**, each acting as a small, fast computer on its own. These processors are interconnected via high-speed networks to ensure rapid communication between them. The **central processing units (CPUs)** and **graphics processing units (GPUs)** in a supercomputer can run in parallel, meaning they work on different parts of the same problem at the same time. This is known as **parallel processing** and is key to a supercomputer's ability to handle massive amounts of data.

Here's a breakdown of how supercomputers work:

1. **Parallel Processing**: Supercomputers divide a complex problem into smaller pieces that can be solved simultaneously. Each processor or core works on a different part of the problem, allowing the supercomputer to tackle incredibly complex tasks much faster than a traditional computer.
2. **High-Speed Networking**: For all those processors to work efficiently, supercomputers are equipped with ultra-fast networks that enable the different parts of the machine to communicate with each other almost instantly.
3. **Data Storage**: Because supercomputers often work with enormous datasets (such as climate models or genetic information), they require **massive storage systems** that can retrieve and store data quickly. Some supercomputers use

**solid-state drives (SSDs)** or other high-speed storage systems to ensure data can be accessed without delay.

4.  **Cooling Systems**: Supercomputers generate a significant amount of heat due to the sheer number of processors working at once. To prevent overheating, they are equipped with advanced **cooling systems**, often involving liquid cooling or specially designed airflow systems.

5.  **Specialized Software**: Supercomputers run on specially designed software that is optimized for parallel processing. This software allows scientists, researchers, and engineers to run simulations, process large datasets, and carry out complex calculations that regular software simply couldn't handle.

## The History of Supercomputers

The concept of supercomputers dates back to the 1960s, when **Seymour Cray**, a pioneering computer architect, designed some of the earliest supercomputers. Cray's designs were revolutionary at the time, focusing on **speed** and **efficiency** to handle scientific problems that standard computers couldn't solve.

1.  **1960s: The Cray-1 Supercomputer**: **Seymour Cray**, known as the father of the supercomputer, developed the **Cray-1** in the 1970s, which became one of the first commercially successful supercomputers. The Cray-1 was designed to be faster than anything else available and introduced new techniques like **vector processing**, which allowed the machine to process large sets of data more efficiently. The Cray-1 was used in **weather forecasting, nuclear research**, and other fields that required vast computational power.

2.  **1980s: Supercomputing Advancements**: Throughout the 1980s, supercomputers evolved with innovations in **parallel computing**. This era saw the development of **massively parallel supercomputers** with thousands of processors working together on a single task. The **Connection Machine**, developed by **Thinking Machines Corporation**, was one of

the first computers to utilize **massive parallelism**, laying the groundwork for the supercomputers of today.

3. **1990s and 2000s: The Growth of Processing Power**: As computing technology advanced, the processing power of supercomputers grew exponentially. Machines like **ASCI Red**, built by **Intel** for the U.S. Department of Energy in the 1990s, could perform over a trillion calculations per second (teraflops), a monumental achievement at the time. By the 2000s, the supercomputing world was dominated by machines capable of **petaflop** performance (quadrillions of calculations per second).

4. **2010s: The Exascale Era**: Today, supercomputers are breaking new boundaries with the advent of **exascale computing**, meaning machines that can perform at least **one exaflop** or a **quintillion calculations per second**. Machines like **China's Sunway TaihuLight** and **IBM's Summit** have broken records in speed and computational power.

## Is Supercomputing Available Now?

Yes, supercomputers are available today, but they are typically operated by **governments**, **research institutions**, **universities**, and **large corporations**. These machines are not for everyday use like a desktop or laptop; rather, they are reserved for tasks that require extreme processing power. For instance, **NASA**, the **U.S. Department of Energy**, and companies like **Google**, **IBM**, and **Microsoft** use supercomputers to carry out **complex simulations**, **scientific research**, and **AI training**.

However, with the rise of **cloud computing**, supercomputing resources are becoming more accessible to businesses and researchers who need high-performance computing but cannot afford to build and maintain a supercomputer. Cloud platforms like **Amazon Web Services (AWS)**, **Google Cloud**, and **Microsoft Azure** offer **supercomputing as a service**, allowing users to access supercomputer power remotely, paying for only what they need.

# The Role of Supercomputers in AI

One of the most significant impacts of supercomputing is in the field of **artificial intelligence (AI)**. AI relies on **machine learning** and **deep learning** algorithms, which often require immense computational resources. Training AI models, particularly in areas like **natural language processing** or **computer vision**, involves processing massive amounts of data, often requiring trillions of calculations. Supercomputers are ideal for these tasks, as they can process data in parallel and reduce the time needed for AI training from weeks or months to just a few days or even hours.

With AI's increasing complexity, supercomputers are essential for **advancing AI research**. They allow for **faster model training, real-time data analysis**, and the development of more sophisticated AI systems. As **AI technology** continues to evolve, supercomputers will play a critical role in making AI more powerful and versatile.

# Supercomputing and the Future

The future of supercomputing is moving toward **exascale computing**. These supercomputers will be capable of performing **quintillions of calculations per second**, enabling new breakthroughs in areas like:

1.  **Healthcare**: Supercomputers are already being used to **model protein folding**, which is essential for developing new treatments for diseases like cancer and Alzheimer's. In the future, they could be instrumental in **personalized medicine**, where treatments are tailored to an individual's unique genetic makeup.
2.  **Space Exploration**: NASA and other space agencies rely on supercomputers to run simulations for everything from rocket launches to **interplanetary travel**. As we push further into space, supercomputing will be essential for navigating the complex physics involved in space exploration.
3.  **Quantum Computing**: While still in its infancy, **quantum computing** represents a possible future direction for

supercomputing. Quantum computers use **qubits** instead of traditional bits, allowing for vastly more efficient computations. If successfully developed, quantum supercomputers could solve problems that today's most powerful supercomputers cannot.

## How Does God Fit into Supercomputing?

Supercomputers, like all technological advancements, reflect the **creative power** and **wisdom** that **God has gifted humanity**. Throughout history, God has inspired innovation in science, technology, and discovery, and supercomputers are no exception. **Proverbs 8:12** says, *"I, wisdom, dwell with prudence, and I find knowledge and discretion."* Supercomputers are tools of knowledge and wisdom, enabling humanity to solve some of the most complex challenges of our time, from curing diseases to understanding the universe.

As we continue to develop these powerful machines, we must remember that **God is the ultimate source of wisdom** and that our innovations should be used to glorify Him and **benefit humanity**. Supercomputing holds immense potential for solving problems that seemed insurmountable just a few decades ago, but it also comes with responsibilities, particularly in the ethical use of technology.

As we move forward, we must seek **God's guidance** in how we apply this technology, ensuring that it serves the **greater good** and reflects His **creative design** in the world. Whether in healthcare, climate science, or artificial intelligence, supercomputers are a gift that can help us better understand and steward the world God has created.

# Chapter 7

## Divine Innovation: God's Hand in Cloud Computing, AI, Supercomputers, and the Creativity of His People

The rise of modern technology—from **cloud computing** and **artificial intelligence (AI)** to **supercomputers**—is one of the greatest testimonies to the **creative power** and **sovereignty** of God. He has gifted humanity with incredible ingenuity, wisdom, and the ability to innovate. These advancements are not mere products of human intellect, but reflections of the divine spark placed within us, fulfilling God's purpose for His creation. The Bible reminds us in **James 1:17** that *"Every good and perfect gift is from above, coming down from the Father of the heavenly lights, who does not change like shifting shadows."* God is the source of all innovation, and through these technological breakthroughs, He is equipping His people to advance His Kingdom in ways that were unimaginable in past centuries.

## Cloud Computing: A Divine Network for God's Kingdom

**Cloud computing** is perhaps one of the most transformative advancements in modern technology. By allowing data and software to be stored and accessed remotely, it enables a **global network of information** sharing and collaboration that transcends physical boundaries. Cloud platforms like **Amazon Web Services (AWS)**,

**Google Cloud**, and **Microsoft Azure** have become essential tools for businesses, governments, and individuals alike. But more importantly, they represent a **divine opportunity** for the **spread of the Gospel**.

The Bible speaks of the power of connectivity and communication in **Proverbs 15:23**, which says, *"A person finds joy in giving an apt reply—and how good is a timely word!"* Cloud computing allows the Gospel to be shared across continents in an instant. Ministries and churches can stream live services to global audiences, provide online Bible studies, and share resources with believers in **closed countries** where Christianity is restricted. This technology is being used to fulfill the Great Commission, as **Matthew 28:19** commands: *"Go and make disciples of all nations, baptizing them in the name of the Father and of the Son and of the Holy Spirit."* Through cloud computing, God is equipping His Church to reach nations that were once unreachable.

Consider how cloud-based services like **YouVersion** have made the Bible accessible to millions worldwide. The **YouVersion Bible app**, powered by cloud technology, offers **hundreds of translations** in dozens of languages, allowing people in remote parts of the world to read Scripture in their native tongue. Even in countries where owning a Bible is illegal, believers can access the Word of God discreetly through cloud-based apps. This is nothing short of a divine miracle, and it demonstrates how God is using modern technology to **overcome obstacles** and bring His Word to every corner of the earth.

In **Acts 1:8**, Jesus tells His disciples, "You will receive power when the Holy Spirit comes on you; and you will be my witnesses in Jerusalem, and in all Judea and Samaria, and to the ends of the earth." Today, cloud computing is one of the most powerful tools the Church has for witnessing "to the ends of the earth." From providing **online church services** to offering **theological education** through distance learning, this technology has broadened the reach of the Gospel like never before. God is clearly at work, orchestrating these technological advancements for His glory and the fulfillment of His divine plan.

# Artificial Intelligence: A Tool for God's Kingdom

**Artificial intelligence (AI)**, though sometimes viewed with skepticism, is another powerful tool that God can use for His purposes. AI systems have already revolutionized industries by providing **solutions to complex problems**, making predictions, and automating processes. But beyond its commercial applications, AI holds immense potential for advancing God's Kingdom.

AI helps us analyze **massive amounts of data**. This means ministries can better understand their communities' needs. They can spot trends early and respond to challenges more efficiently. God is using AI to help His Church work smarter in reaching people for Christ. AI can help churches and organizations tailor their **outreach efforts**, ensuring that they reach the right people at the right time with the right message. Imagine an AI-powered tool that can sift through global data to identify areas where the Gospel is spreading quickly and areas where more evangelistic efforts are needed. AI can be used to enhance **missions' strategy**, allowing us to work smarter, not harder, for the Kingdom.

The potential of AI extends even further into **Bible translation**. AI-driven translation tools are being used to accelerate the translation of the Bible into **unreached languages**, fulfilling the prophecy of **Revelation 7:9**, which speaks of a great multitude from every nation, tribe, people, and language worshiping before the throne of God. As **Isaiah 55:11** declares, *"So shall my word be that goes out from my mouth; it shall not return to me empty, but it shall accomplish that which I purpose and shall succeed in the thing for which I sent it."* Through AI, God's Word is being translated faster than ever before, ensuring that His purpose is fulfilled in every nation and language.

Additionally, AI tools can assist in **apologetics** and **evangelism**, helping believers answer difficult questions and objections with speed and accuracy. Imagine an AI-driven app that provides **real-time apologetic responses** to questions about the Bible, theology, and Christianity—empowering believers to witness more effectively. As **1**

**Peter 3:15** instructs, *"Always be prepared to give an answer to everyone who asks you to give the reason for the hope that you have."* AI can help equip Christians to fulfill this command more effectively, allowing them to respond to seekers and skeptics alike with **wisdom** and **truth**.

## Supercomputers: Unleashing God's Knowledge for His Glory

**Supercomputers** represent the pinnacle of computational power, capable of performing **trillions of calculations per second**. These machines are used in fields ranging from **climate science** to **molecular modeling** to **space exploration**. But beyond their scientific applications, supercomputers have immense potential for **Kingdom work**.

One of the most exciting possibilities is the use of supercomputers in **Biblical archaeology** and **textual analysis**. By processing massive datasets, supercomputers can help uncover **historical evidence** that supports the truth of Scripture. For instance, supercomputers can analyze **ancient manuscripts** to reveal subtle variations in Biblical texts, helping scholars better understand the original meaning of Scripture. As **Jeremiah 33:3** promises, *"Call to me and I will answer you and tell you great and unsearchable things you do not know."* Supercomputers are helping to unlock these "unsearchable things," giving us deeper insight into God's Word and its historical context.

Furthermore, as **quantum computing**—the next generation of supercomputing—becomes a reality, we may soon have the ability to process information in ways that were previously unimaginable. Quantum computers, which use qubits instead of traditional bits, have the potential to **revolutionize fields like cryptography**, **genetics**, and **material science**. But for the Church, quantum computing represents a new frontier for understanding the **complexity of God's creation**. As scientists explore the quantum world, we are reminded of **Psalm 139:6**, which says, *"Such knowledge is too wonderful for me; it is high; I cannot attain it."* Quantum computing will reveal even more about the intricate design of the universe, pointing us back to the majesty and wisdom of God.

## The Creativity of God's People: Reflecting the Divine Creator

God has always worked through His people to bring about **innovative solutions** for the challenges facing the world. The **creativity** we see in the development of software, apps, cloud computing, AI, and supercomputers reflects the **image of God** within us. **Genesis 1:27** tells us that we are made in the image of God, and just as God is the ultimate Creator, we, too, are called to **create**, **innovate**, and **build**.

Throughout history, God has raised up **inventors**, **scientists**, and **technologists** who have used their God-given talents to bless the world. From **Isaac Newton** discovering the laws of gravity to **Charles Babbage** conceptualizing the first computer, God has always worked through His people to bring about breakthroughs that advance His purposes. **Colossians 1:16-17** reminds us, *"For in Him all things were created: things in heaven and on earth, visible and invisible... all things have been created through Him and for Him. He is before all things, and in Him all things hold together."* Every piece of technology—whether it be a supercomputer or a smartphone—exists because God allowed it to come into existence, and it all works together for His glory.

Today, the creative power of God's people is on full display in the development of apps that serve the Kingdom. Apps like **Blue Letter Bible**, Bible Hub, **Bible Project**, or even Strongs Concordance, and **Glorify** have made **discipleship** and **Bible study** accessible to millions. These apps are not just tools for convenience; they are tools for **transformation**, bringing God's Word to people who might never step foot in a church. As the Church embraces these technologies, we are fulfilling the call of **Matthew 5:14**, where Jesus says, *"You are the light of the world. A city set on a hill cannot be hidden."* Through technology, we are shining the light of Christ into every corner of the globe, bringing hope, healing, and salvation to a lost world.

# God's Sovereign Plan: Working All Things for His Glory

As we look at the technological advancements of the 21st century, we must remember that **God is sovereign** over all things. **Romans 8:28** assures us that *"in all things God works for the good of those who love him, who have been called according to his purpose."* This includes the tools and technologies that have been developed in recent years. Whether it's cloud computing enabling global collaboration, AI driving innovation in missions, or supercomputers revealing the intricacies of God's creation, God is using all of it to fulfill His plan.

We may not always understand how these technologies fit into God's greater strategy, but we can trust that He is at work. **Isaiah 55:8-9** reminds us, *"For my thoughts are not your thoughts, neither are your ways my ways... As the heavens are higher than the earth, so are my ways higher than your ways and my thoughts than your thoughts."* God's plan is far greater than anything we can imagine, and He is using these advancements to bring about the **salvation of souls**, the **growth of His Church**, and the **transformation of lives**.

As we continue to develop and use these tools, we must do so with the knowledge that **all of creation exists for God's glory**. Every invention, every algorithm, and every breakthrough is an opportunity to **reflect His creativity**, **wisdom**, and **love**. Let us use these gifts to advance His Kingdom, bringing hope to the hopeless and light to those in darkness. In everything we do, let us remember **Colossians 3:17**: *"And whatever you do, whether in word or deed, do it all in the name of the Lord Jesus, giving thanks to God the Father through him."* Through technology, God is working to accomplish His will, and we are privileged to be part of His plan.

These technologies aren't just theoretical, they're already shaping how we share God's love. Let me show you what this might look like in the near future, through the story of some faithful innovators who learned to use these tools for God's glory.

# Story Time

## A Journey Through the Divine Blueprint: The Story of Technology and God's Plan

In the year 2040, the world had changed. Technology had evolved far beyond what anyone in the 20th century could have imagined, and with it came both immense opportunity and great responsibility. The convergence of **cloud computing**, **artificial intelligence (AI)**, **supercomputers**, and **quantum computing** has transformed every aspect of life—commerce, healthcare, communication, and education. However, it was in the lives of **believers** where the true potential of these tools began to unfold, revealing a deeper purpose within God's plan for humanity.

The story begins in a bustling, vibrant city called **New Haven**, where technology has become intertwined with everyday life. Among the city's inhabitants were a group of believers who had come together with a shared vision: to use the power of these new technologies to bring **God's light** into a world filled with confusion, distraction, and digital overload. They called themselves the **New Creators**, drawing inspiration from **Ephesians 2:10**, which says, *"For we are God's handiwork, created in Christ Jesus to do good works, which God prepared in advance for us to do."* This group believed that God had prepared this moment in history—this technological era—for a purpose. And their mission was to walk with the **Holy Spirit**, listening step by step for His guidance as they navigated this new world.

## The Call to Innovation

The New Creators were led by **David**, a humble yet brilliant computer scientist who had grown up fascinated by the potential of technology but was always sensitive to the **Holy Spirit's guidance** in how it should be used. David understood that technology, like any tool, could either be used for good or for harm, depending on the heart of the person wielding it. **Proverbs 3:5-6** had always been his guiding verse:

*"Trust in the Lord with all your heart and lean not on your own understanding; in all your ways submit to him, and he will make your paths straight."* He knew that in order to use technology for God's glory, he had to lean not on human wisdom but on God's.

David was surrounded by a team of individuals, each with their own unique gifts and talents. **Sarah**, a gifted AI researcher, had developed algorithms that could analyze human behavior in ways that made communication and learning more intuitive. **Isaac**, a quantum computing expert, had been working on creating algorithms that could solve some of the world's greatest scientific problems in mere seconds. **Rebecca**, a cloud architect, had built systems that could store and process unimaginable amounts of data securely, ensuring that the church and ministries could expand their global reach without ever being compromised. And **Lucas**, a young developer with a passion for justice, had designed apps to help believers connect across the world for prayer, Bible study, and outreach.

As they met one evening in their small office overlooking the city, David felt a deep sense of purpose rise within him. "God is showing us the blueprint," he said to his team. "We've been given these tools, and it's no coincidence. The enemy is using technology to sow division, confusion, and distraction, but **God** has always been steps ahead. We've been called to use these innovations to create platforms of unity, truth, and light."

David opened his Bible to **Isaiah 43:19**, which had been on his heart that day: *"See, I am doing a new thing! Now it springs up; do you not perceive it? I am making a way in the wilderness and streams in the wasteland."* He looked around at his team and continued, "I believe God is calling us to create 'streams in the wasteland'—to build networks, apps, and platforms that will not only share the Gospel but will transform how believers live out their faith in this digital world."

# The Power of Cloud Computing

Rebecca was the first to speak up. "I've been working on something," she said. "I believe **cloud computing** is a gift from God to help unify His people across the world. We've already seen how ministries are using it to stream sermons, hold virtual Bible studies, and share resources. But what if we could take it further?"

Rebecca shared her vision for a **global cloud-based platform** that would allow believers from every corner of the earth to **collaborate** in real-time on mission projects, prayer meetings, and discipleship training. This platform would be encrypted and secure, ensuring that even in countries where Christianity was restricted, believers could safely connect and share their faith without fear of persecution.

"We could build a cloud-based **prayer network**," she said excitedly. "A place where believers could submit prayer requests, intercede for one another, and see real-time updates of answered prayers. Imagine watching the Church move and grow globally in real-time! **1 Thessalonians 5:17** says to 'pray continually,' and I believe God is giving us the tools to make that a reality for the whole body of Christ."

David smiled, knowing that Rebecca's heart was aligned with God's vision. "I can see it now," he said. "A cloud that doesn't just store information but stores **intercession**. We can create something that lets believers from all over the world lift each other up in prayer, in unity."

# The Potential of Artificial Intelligence

Next, Sarah stepped forward. "AI has incredible potential, but I think we've only scratched the surface of how it can be used for God's purposes," she said. "Right now, AI is mostly used for consumerism, for predicting what people want to buy, watch, or eat. But what if we could train AI to **help people understand Scripture** in a deeper way?"

Sarah had been working on a project she called **ScriptureSense**, an AI-powered tool that could read and analyze the Bible in real-time, offering **insights** and **cross-references** to related verses, historical context, and theological commentary. It was designed to be an **interactive Bible study assistant**, but Sarah believed it could go further.

"What if AI could identify **spiritual needs** based on the content of people's prayers and connect them with believers who've gone through similar experiences?" she proposed. "For instance, someone struggling with **fear** could be connected with those who have overcome fear through **faith** and Scripture. It would be like a digital form of **discipleship**, connecting the right people at the right time."

David nodded. "AI can be used to strengthen the **global Church** by helping believers grow in their knowledge of God's Word," he said. "And more than that, it can be a tool to bring **healing** and **encouragement**. Imagine AI not only answering **doctrinal questions** but leading people into **Holy Spirit-guided** prayer. The Bible says in **Romans 8:26**, 'The Spirit helps us in our weakness. We do not know what we ought to pray for, but the Spirit himself intercedes for us through wordless groans.' AI, under the direction of God's people, could help facilitate deeper prayer lives for believers all over the world."

## The Unimaginable Power of Supercomputers

Isaac, who had been quiet so far, leaned forward. "I've been thinking about supercomputers," he said. "We've been using them to model weather patterns, simulate drug interactions, and even explore the cosmos. But what if **supercomputers** could be used for something even greater? Something more eternal?"

Isaac shared his vision for using supercomputers to **accelerate Bible translation**. "Right now, there are over **7,000 languages** in the world, and many of them still don't have a complete Bible translation. Supercomputers can process **millions of data points** at once. What if we fed them all the linguistic data we have and used them to translate the Bible into every language within a matter of months, not decades?"

David's eyes widened. "That could be the fulfillment of **Revelation 7:9**," he said. "A great multitude from every nation, tribe, people, and language, standing before the throne and before the Lamb. If we could accelerate translation efforts, we might see the **Great Commission** fulfilled in our lifetime."

Isaac nodded, excited. "Supercomputers could also help us **map out** unreached people groups, analyzing global data to find places where the Gospel hasn't yet reached. We could then use that information to **strategically** send missionaries, equipped with translations in their native languages, backed by the power of cloud computing and AI."

David smiled. "God is truly doing something **new**. He's giving us the ability to use technology to bring the **Word of God** to every corner of the earth."

## Quantum Computing: A Glimpse of God's Unsearchable Wisdom

But Isaac wasn't finished. "There's more," he said. "Quantum computing is the future. It's unlike anything we've seen before. With **quantum computers**, we won't just process information faster—we'll be able to solve problems that are currently **unsolvable**. Think of it as getting a glimpse of **God's unsearchable wisdom**."

David leaned in, curious. "What do you mean?"

Isaac explained how quantum computers could revolutionize **cryptography**, ensuring secure communications for missionaries in restricted nations. He talked about how they could unlock new **medical discoveries**, offering cures for diseases that have plagued humanity for centuries. But most of all, Isaac saw quantum computing as a way to explore the **intricacies of God's creation**—to better understand the mysteries of the universe that point directly to the Creator.

"**Psalm 139:6** says, 'Such knowledge is too wonderful for me; it is high; I cannot attain it.' Quantum computing will reveal things about **God's creation** that are too high for us to attain now, but as we unlock these mysteries, we'll come face to face with **God's glory**."

## Walking Step by Step with the Holy Spirit

As the evening went on, the New Creators began to pray together, asking God for **wisdom** and **guidance** in their mission. They knew that the power of technology could either be used to build up the **Kingdom of God** or be used for selfish gain and destruction. But they were determined to walk **step by step** with the **Holy Spirit**, trusting Him to lead them every step of the way.

**Romans 8:14** became their guiding verse: *"For those who are led by the Spirit of God are the children of God."* They knew that they couldn't rely on their own understanding. Each decision—each line of code, each algorithm, each design—needed to be submitted to the **Holy Spirit**.

And so, the New Creators began their work. They built the **prayer cloud**, connecting believers across the world in real-time intercession. They developed **ScriptureSense**, using AI to help believers grow deeper in their knowledge of the Word. They deployed supercomputers to accelerate Bible translations and sent missionaries equipped with quantum-encrypted technology into the most remote parts of the world.

## A Glimpse of God's Future

As the years went on, the world began to change. The tools of the digital age—once used for consumerism, distraction, and division—were now being used to **build the Kingdom of God**. The **Church** became more connected, more informed, and more united than ever before. The Gospel was being spread to every tribe, tongue, and nation, and the **Great Commission** was coming closer to fulfillment.

And through it all, God's hand was evident. He was leading His people—step by step, through every advancement, every breakthrough, and every challenge. **Proverbs 16:9** echoed in their hearts: *"In their hearts humans plan their course, but the Lord establishes their steps."*

The New Creators knew that they were part of something much greater than themselves. They were part of God's divine plan—using the gifts He had given them to **shine His light** into the world. They were using technology, not for their own gain, but to bring **glory to God** and to lead people into a deeper relationship with the **Creator of all things**.

In the end, they understood that technology was just a tool—a tool that could either be used for good or for evil. But in their hands, led by the **Holy Spirit**, it became a tool for **transformation**, for **hope**, and for the **advancement of God's Kingdom**.

And as the **global Church** continued to grow, they knew that the best was yet to come. **God** was still at work, and the future—no matter how advanced, no matter how digital—was firmly in His hands.

## Conclusion of Part 2: The Rise of Computers and Software as Tools of God's Plan

As we conclude this powerful exploration of how computers, software, and networks have risen under God's orchestration, it becomes clear that we are living in an era of divine innovation. God's fingerprints are on every technological advancement, and what might seem like mere human invention is, in fact, part of His larger, eternal blueprint.

From the mechanical visions of Charles Babbage to the cryptographic brilliance of Alan Turing, we've seen how God imparted wisdom to key figures in the development of computers. He gave them the insight and knowledge needed to birth a new era of information processing and communication. The rise of software has similarly been an unfolding of God's plan, allowing humanity to create tools that empower, connect, and bring His truth to every corner of the world.

Now, the question remains—how will you be a part of this story?

God has set the stage. The same power that birthed computing is still at work today, calling His people to use these tools for His Kingdom. As we've learned, these advancements are not accidental—they are opportunities divinely given for the spread of the Gospel, for deeper connection among believers, and for the creation of systems that reflect God's order and creativity.

It's time to step forward into this grand vision. Just as God used Babbage, Turing, and von Neumann, He is ready to use you. Whether you are a technologist, a creator, a leader, or simply someone seeking to make an impact in this digital age, you are part of this divine plan. The same Spirit that inspired the creators of the past is with you now, guiding your steps into the future.

## Call to Action

Ask yourself—how can you use the gifts God has given you to advance His Kingdom through technology? How can you ensure that your work reflects His wisdom and purpose?

Perhaps it's developing software that brings people closer to Christ. Maybe it's creating networks that connect believers across the world in unity. Or it might be as simple as using your everyday tech to share the Gospel and inspire hope.

The tools are in your hands, and the possibilities are endless. Let's not allow the enemy to twist technology for harm but instead claim it for God's glory. Together, we can build platforms of connection, systems of truth, and networks of prayer that transform the world.

**Step into divine innovation!** Seek the Holy Spirit's guidance in all that you do and watch how God will use your work to impact eternity. The future is bright, and we are called to be light bearers in a world that desperately needs it.

God's divine innovation is alive and well—what role will you play in this unfolding story? Step out in faith, create, innovate, and trust that God is leading you to something far greater than you could ever imagine. **The world is waiting, and the time is now.**

Let's build the future together, one that glorifies God and furthers His eternal plan!

# Part 3

# Technology the Battling Evil Harnessing God's Gifts: Technology, Innovation, and Spiritual Warfare

# Walking with God Through the Digital Era: Protecting and Advancing His Kingdom While Facing the Enemy's Schemes

In this section, *Harnessing God's Gifts: Technology, Innovation, and Spiritual Warfare,* we explore the profound connection between the digital age and the spiritual battles that believers face today. Technology, like all of God's gifts, holds immense potential to advance His Kingdom and bless humanity, but it also presents new opportunities for the enemy to deceive, distract, and destroy. From the Industrial Revolution to today's breakthroughs in cloud computing, artificial intelligence, and supercomputers, we see how God has always equipped His people with tools for innovation and progress. Yet, the enemy is ever at work, seeking to corrupt and misuse these advancements. As believers, we are called to walk step by step with the Holy Spirit, discerning how to use technology for God's purposes while standing against the enemy's schemes. This section will guide you through recognizing the spiritual conflict that underlies technological advancements and provide insight into how to stand firm in God's truth amidst a rapidly evolving digital landscape.

# Chapter 8

## Walking Step by Step with God: Harnessing Technology for His Plan and Facing the Enemy

God's creation is full of wonders, and **technology** is no exception. It represents a beautiful fusion of human ingenuity and divine inspiration, revealing the power of walking step by step with **God's plan**. When His people listen, follow His guidance, and walk in obedience to His Spirit, they accomplish remarkable things. Whether through the **Industrial Revolution** or the modern-day explosion of **cloud computing**, **AI**, and **supercomputing**, God uses His people to bless, provide for, and protect His beloved children.

The story of the Industrial Revolution reminds us that God, in His wisdom, led humanity into an era of unprecedented **innovation** and **growth**. He provided the **knowledge** and **resources** to build machinery, transport goods, and improve lives. As God says in **Isaiah 28:26**, *"His God instructs him and teaches him the right way."* It was through His instruction that humanity learned to harness the forces of nature, turning steam and coal into energy and using machinery to produce goods on a mass scale.

God used the **Industrial Revolution** to **provide** for His people. Factories produced textiles, food, and essential goods more efficiently, helping to clothe and feed the poor. **Railways** connected distant towns, enabling the spread of commerce and community. These developments brought **prosperity** and **opportunity** to countless families who had been struggling to survive. **God's covenant** to provide for His people was evident as industries boomed, and the fruits of innovation were shared.

Yet, we must also acknowledge that **great evil** was present during this time. The **enemy**, ever opposed to God's plan, sought to **corrupt** the good that God had initiated. With the rise of factories came **exploitation**—child labor, unsafe working conditions, and the abuse of workers for profit. The very tools that had been created to **bless humanity** were, in many cases, misused for **greed** and **oppression**.

But God, in His mercy, raised up faithful servants who stood against these injustices. **William Wilberforce**, a Christian politician, fought tirelessly for the abolition of slavery during the Industrial Revolution. His work helped free millions from bondage. Similarly, **Elizabeth Fry** advocated for prison reform, helping to ensure more humane treatment for inmates. These were individuals walking step by step with the **Holy Spirit**, hearing God's voice, and doing His will. They worked to **redeem** what the enemy had sought to destroy.

**Proverbs 31:8-9** reminds us of our responsibility to act against evil: *"Speak up for those who cannot speak for themselves, for the rights of all who are destitute. Speak up and judge fairly; defend the rights of the poor and needy."* God raised up men and women to defend the defenseless during the Industrial Revolution, and He is doing the same today in the face of **modern technology**. Just as believers were called to fight against the **darkness** during the Industrial Revolution, they are now being called to fight against the enemy's attempts to corrupt **technology** in the 21st century.

## God's New Creation: Technology Today

With the rise of **cloud computing**, **artificial intelligence**, and **supercomputers**, we are witnessing another massive shift in how humanity interacts with the world around us. These tools offer unprecedented **power** and **possibility** for good, but they also present new dangers if misused.

As **believers**, we are called to recognize the potential of these technologies to **advance God's Kingdom**, but also to stay alert to the **enemy's schemes**. 1 Peter 5:8 warns us, *"Be alert and of sober mind. Your enemy the devil prowls around like a roaring lion looking for someone to devour."* The enemy will always seek to **corrupt** what God has given as good, and technology is no exception.

**Cloud computing**, for example, enables the sharing of **God's Word** to millions across the globe. Ministries can store and stream vast amounts of **Christian content**—sermons, teachings, worship services—reaching even those in **restricted nations**. The development of platforms like **YouVersion** allows people worldwide to access the Bible in their own languages, fulfilling God's promise in **Isaiah 55:11**: *"My word that goes out from my mouth will not return to me empty, but will accomplish what I desire and achieve the purpose for which I sent it."*

But the same cloud infrastructure can be misused for **evil purposes**— from hosting illegal material to facilitating cybercrimes. The enemy would love nothing more than to twist this **gift** of connectivity into a tool of deception and destruction.

**Artificial intelligence (AI)** is another area where **God's divine creativity** is evident. With AI, we can create tools that analyze **Scripture**, offer **discipleship** resources, and translate the Bible into every language in the world. But AI can also be used to create **misinformation**, manipulate emotions, or spread harmful content.

Similarly, **supercomputers** offer the Church unprecedented power. These machines can help us solve problems that have baffled humanity for generations. From **accelerating Bible translation** to **predicting natural disasters** and preparing for them, these tools can bless humanity in ways we are only beginning to understand. **Quantum computing**, with its ability to perform unimaginable calculations, will open doors to understanding God's creation in even deeper ways. **Isaiah 40:28** declares, *"Do you not know? Have you not heard? The Lord is the everlasting God, the Creator of the ends of the earth. He will not grow tired or weary, and his understanding no one* *can fathom.*" Supercomputing is merely a glimpse of that divine understanding.

But again, the enemy lurks, eager to twist what God has made for good. **Surveillance, autonomous weapons**, and **mass data collection** are some technologies that can be used for good in some cases but can be extremely destructive in the enemy's hands. These have just come off the dark path's technology can take if placed in the wrong hands.

## Walking Step by Step with the Holy Spirit

As believers, we must remain grounded in **God's Word** and walk in step with the **Holy Spirit**. This means **seeking God's wisdom** before we create, build, or innovate. **James 1:5** reminds us, *"If any of you lacks wisdom, you should ask God, who gives generously to all without finding fault, and it will be given to you."* The Holy Spirit will guide us in how to use these **technological advancements** for the glory of God, for the **good of His people**, and to further His Kingdom.

## The Enemy's Plan: Corrupting God's Creation

As we step into this era of technological innovation, we must understand that Satan, the enemy of God's people, is always working to **destroy, corrupt**, and **pervert** what God has created for good. From the beginning, Satan has sought to thwart God's plan. In the **Garden of Eden**, he deceived Adam and Eve, leading them into sin. In the **wilderness**, he tempted Jesus with power and control. And today, he seeks to use the very tools God has given humanity— technology, creativity, and innovation—to lead us astray.

The enemy's ultimate goal is to **separate** people from God and His purposes. He uses **greed, pride**, and **lust for power** to corrupt what could be used for **good**. During the Industrial Revolution, the enemy capitalized on **human greed** to exploit workers, create unsafe conditions, and turn innovation into a tool of **oppression**. Today, the same temptations exist in the technological realm. **Data manipulation, addictive social media algorithms**, and **deep fake**

**technology** are just some examples of how the enemy uses technology to ensnare humanity.

But we know that **God is sovereign**, and His plan will not be thwarted. **John 10:10** declares, *"The thief comes only to steal and kill and destroy; I have come that they may have life and have it to the full."* Jesus offers us a way out of the enemy's trap, and He empowers us to use technology for **good**—for **justice**, **mercy**, and the **advancement of the Gospel**.

## The Battle for Technology: God's Plan for Redemption

Today's tech leaders face similar choices to those factory owners did. A social media company can either protect user privacy or exploit personal data. An AI developer can create algorithms that help or harm. The same battles for justice and ethics continue, they've just moved from factories to server farms. Just as **Wilberforce** fought against slavery and **Elizabeth Fry** worked for prison reform during the Industrial Revolution, believers today are called to **redeem technology** from the enemy's grip. We are called to **speak up**, to **create**, and to build systems that reflect God's love and justice.

God is calling His people to step into the **digital battleground** with **boldness** and **confidence**. He is equipping His Church with the tools of **AI**, **cloud computing**, and **supercomputers**, not just to advance human knowledge but to **reclaim what the enemy has stolen**.

**Romans 8:28** reminds us, *"And we know that in all things God works for the good of those who love him, who have been called according to his purpose."* Even as the enemy seeks to destroy, God is **redeeming**. Even as the enemy tries to pervert, God is **restoring**. His plans will prevail, and His people—walking step by step with the Holy Spirit—will carry out His purposes through the very technology that the enemy intends to twist.

But we don't just study the enemy to fear him. We study him to defeat him. God has already won the victory through Christ, and He's equipped us with both spiritual armor and practical wisdom to protect His creation. Let's look at God's strategy for redeeming technology.

## The Divine Strategy

As we move further into this **technological era**, we must remember that **God is the ultimate Creator**. **Cloud computing**, **AI**, **supercomputers**, and **quantum computing** are all tools that God has placed in the hands of His people to **build**, **restore**, and **expand His Kingdom**. **Ephesians 3:20** says, *"Now to him who is able to do immeasurably more than all we ask or imagine, according to his power that is at work within us."* The potential is limitless when we walk in step with God's Spirit.

Let us be bold in **creating**, faithful in **praying**, and diligent in **seeking** His will as we move forward. God is always **leading**, and His plan will always come to fruition—even in the face of the enemy's schemes. With God, technology becomes not just a tool for progress but a weapon for **redemption**, and we, His people, are called to be part of this **divine strategy**.

**Proverbs 16:3** sums it up perfectly: *"Commit to the Lord whatever you do, and he will establish your plans."* As we walk with Him, there is no limit to what God can do through His people and His creation.

## Educating Ourselves About the Enemy: Exposing His Strategies to Protect God's Creations

As believers, we are not only called to celebrate the **wonders of God's creations** but also to be aware of the **enemy** who seeks to use these same creations to **destroy** and **mislead**. The Bible teaches us that **Satan**, the enemy of God's people, is a master of deception, working tirelessly to corrupt what God has created for good. **John 10:10** reminds us of this clearly: *"The thief comes only to steal and kill and destroy; I have come that they may have life and have it to the full."*

We must do more than just acknowledge the enemy exists. We need to **shine light** on the **enemy's strategies** and strip away his **power** to deceive. When we understand how he works, we can better defend God's people and protect His gifts. **powerless. Ephesians 6:11** tells us, *"Put on the full armor of God, so that you can take your stand against the devil's schemes."* By understanding the strategies Satan uses and the reasons behind them, we can be better equipped to defend against them, knowing that with the **power of Christ**, the enemy is already defeated.

# Chapter 9

## Who is the Enemy?  How is he causing issues for us through Technology?

Every time you unlock your phone, you're stepping onto a battlefield. That might sound dramatic, but it's true. An enemy waits to twist technology against you - the same enemy who has fought against God's people throughout history. You might know him as Satan, or the Devil. Once he was Lucifer, a high-ranking angel who let pride destroy him. Isaiah 14:12-14 describes his fall from heaven when he tried to set himself above God. Now he works to corrupt everything good that God creates, including our modern technology.

Satan, or the Devil, formerly known as **Lucifer**, was once a high-ranking angel in God's kingdom. But his heart became filled with **pride,** and he desired to place himself above God. His rebellion resulted in his being cast out of heaven, along with a third of the angels who followed him. **Isaiah 14:12-14** describes this fall: *"How you have fallen from heaven, morning star, son of the dawn! You have been cast down to the earth... You said in your heart, 'I will ascend to the heavens; I will raise my throne above the stars of God.'"* From that moment, Satan became the **adversary**, constantly working against God and His people.

Satan's primary motivation is to **corrupt** and **destroy** what God has created. He is filled with hatred toward God and seeks to **distract** humanity from God's purposes. He desires to **steal** our peace, **kill** our joy, and **destroy** our hope. Yet, he is not a creator—he can only pervert what already exists, twisting good things into evil uses.

# The Enemy's Strategy: Using Technology for Destruction

Just as Satan used the **fruit of the Tree of Knowledge** to deceive Adam and Eve in the Garden of Eden, he seeks to **misuse** God's creations today. As technology advances, so does Satan's attempt to twist it for his dark purposes. The **Industrial Revolution** brought about incredible growth and prosperity, but the enemy also used it to foster **greed**, **exploitation**, and **oppression**. Now, as we step into an age dominated by **cloud computing**, **AI**, and **supercomputers**, Satan will seek to **corrupt** these tools in the same way.

Let's explore some of the specific **strategies** the enemy uses with modern technology, and how we, as believers, can shine light on them.

### 1.  The Strategy of Deception and Manipulation

One of Satan's primary strategies is **deception**. He is the father of lies, as Jesus calls him in **John 8:44**: *"When he lies, he speaks his native language, for he is a liar and the father of lies."* In the digital world, deception can take many forms—misinformation, false identities, and fake narratives being spread across the internet at lightning speed. **Artificial intelligence** and social media algorithms are often manipulated to spread false information that confuses and deceives people.

Deepfakes, for example, are AI-generated videos or images that can make someone appear to say or do things they never did. The potential for **manipulation** is enormous, and the enemy's goal is to use this technology to create **chaos** and **distrust**. Imagine how Satan can use false images, audio, and videos to **undermine** truth and **sow division**.

Our defense against this is to **stand firm in the truth** of God's Word. **John 8:32** says, *"Then you will know the truth, and the truth will set you free."* As believers, we must be diligent in seeking the truth and **discerning** what we see and hear in the digital world. This is why the

**Holy Spirit** is so critical in our lives. He leads us into all truth, as Jesus promised in **John 16:13**: *"But when he, the Spirit of truth, comes, he will guide you into all the truth."* With His guidance, we can expose the enemy's lies and walk confidently in the light.

### 2.   The Strategy of Distraction

Satan's second major strategy is **distraction**. In today's fast-paced world, filled with constant notifications, social media feeds, and 24-hour news cycles, it's easy to become distracted from **God's plan** for our lives. The enemy uses technology to flood our minds with **noise**, leaving us no space to hear God's voice. He knows that if he can keep us busy, scrolling endlessly on our devices, we won't have time to reflect on God's Word, to pray, or to hear from the Holy Spirit.

Jesus spoke about this in **Luke 10:41-42** when He told Martha, "Martha, Martha, you are worried and upset about many things, but few things are needed—or indeed only one. Mary has chosen what is better, and it will not be taken away from her." In a world filled with distractions, we must be like Mary, sitting at the feet of Jesus and listening to His voice.

Our **defense** against distraction is to be **intentional** about spending time with God. We must prioritize our relationship with Him above all else. **Romans 12:2** commands us, *"Do not conform to the pattern of this world, but be transformed by the renewing of your mind."* By renewing our minds through God's Word and **quieting** the distractions of technology, we can hear God's voice clearly and avoid the enemy's trap.

### 3.   The Strategy of Division

Another of Satan's primary tactics is **division**. The enemy thrives on creating conflict and separation among people—whether through political arguments, social divides, or even denominational disputes within the Church. **AI algorithms** on social media platforms can be manipulated to show people only the content that reinforces their pre-existing beliefs, further dividing people into **tribalism** and **isolation**.

The enemy will use these platforms to sow discord and hatred, making it harder for people to **love** one another as Christ commanded.

**Mark 3:25** says, *"If a house is divided against itself, that house cannot stand."* Satan understands this truth and works to divide us— whether it's in our families, our churches, or our communities.

To fight this strategy, we must be **peacemakers**, walking in **love** and **unity** as Christ has called us to do. **Colossians 3:14** urges, *"And over all these virtues put on love, which binds them all together in perfect unity."* The Church is uniquely positioned to use technology as a **tool of reconciliation**, bringing people together instead of allowing the enemy to divide us. **Ephesians 4:3** reminds us to be **"eager to maintain the unity of the Spirit in the bond of peace."**

### 4. The Strategy of Exploitation

Satan's fourth strategy is **exploitation**. During the **Industrial Revolution**, we saw how human beings were exploited for profit— workers forced to labor in unsafe conditions for minimal pay. Today, the enemy's goal is to **exploit technology**. **Human trafficking**, **cybercrimes**, and **digital addiction** are all ways that people are being abused through modern advancements. The enemy desires to see **God's image-bearers** enslaved by their devices, addicted to pornography, gambling, or social media, never experiencing the **freedom** that God offers.

The addictive nature of social media and internet use goes beyond simple habit formation. These platforms are specifically engineered to trigger your brain's reward system through the release of dopamine - the same chemical involved in other forms of addiction. Each notification, like, or piece of novel information provides a small dopamine hit, creating a powerful chemical dependency.

This isn't just psychological - it's a physical reaction that makes breaking free from internet addiction particularly challenging. The enemy understands this biological vulnerability and uses these platforms to keep us trapped in cycles of dependency, pulling us away from God's purposes for our lives.

But, Jesus came to set the captives free. **Isaiah 61:1** says, *"He has sent me to bind up the brokenhearted, to proclaim freedom for the captives and release from darkness for the prisoners."* As the Church, we must stand against the exploitation of vulnerable people. Whether it's advocating for stronger regulations to protect children online or providing counseling to those suffering from **digital addiction**, we are called to bring freedom in Christ to those who are oppressed.

### 5. The Strategy of Isolation

Lastly, Satan seeks to **isolate** us. He knows that when believers are **disconnected** from the body of Christ, they are more vulnerable to his attacks. **Hebrews 10:25** warns us, *"Do not give up meeting together, as some are in the habit of doing, but encouraging one another—and all the more as you see the Day approaching."* While technology can connect us, the enemy will try to use it to create **virtual worlds** where people no longer have meaningful relationships.

We see this in the rise of **virtual realities** and **online identities**, where people may feel "connected" through their devices but are, in fact, becoming more isolated from real, flesh-and-blood communities. The Church must work against this strategy by using technology to **foster true community**, encouraging believers to gather in-person and online in meaningful ways.

**Let's look in more detail who the enemy is and why he is doing what he is doing.**

# Chapter: 10

## The Fall and Redemption of Humanity; A Story of Dominion

### Creation, Fall, and Redemption

In the beginning, when God created Adam, He granted humanity **complete dominion** over the earth, as seen in **Genesis 1:28**, where God commands Adam to "fill the earth and subdue it." This authority symbolized God's trust in humanity to **govern** and **steward** His creation in partnership with Him. The Garden of Eden housed two key trees: the **Tree of Life**, which symbolized ongoing communion and eternal life with God, and the **Tree of the Knowledge of Good and Evil**, representing the choice of moral autonomy—living according to human will, independent from God's guidance.

However, Adam and Eve's decision to eat from the Tree of the Knowledge of Good and Evil, tempted by the serpent (Satan), resulted in the **Fall**. By disobeying God's direct command, they introduced **sin** and **death** into the world and handed over the dominion God had entrusted to them to the Devil (Genesis 3:1-6). As a result, the perfect relationship between humanity and God was broken, and all of creation fell under the curse of sin (Romans 5:12). The consequences of the Fall were devastating, bringing **toil**, **pain**, and **death** to humanity and the world they were meant to steward.

Yet, even in humanity's disobedience, **God's love** remained unshakable. Rather than abandon His creation, God immediately set in motion a plan for **redemption**. In **Genesis 3:15**, God promised that a descendant of Eve would crush the serpent's head, symbolizing the ultimate defeat of Satan. This prophetic promise pointed to **Jesus**

**Christ**, God's Son, who would come into the world as the **Redeemer**, offering salvation to all of humanity. Through His perfect life, death, and resurrection, Jesus would reclaim the dominion that was lost, restoring the relationship between God and His creation.

Throughout the **Old Testament**, God revealed pieces of His plan through **covenants** and **prophecies**, most notably His covenant with **Abraham**, promising that through his descendants, "all nations will be blessed" (Genesis 12:3). This pointed toward the coming of the Messiah, **Jesus Christ**, who fulfilled over 300 prophecies. The **New Testament** reveals that Jesus' death on the cross provided atonement for the sins of humanity, freeing all who believe in Him from the power of sin and death (Romans 6:23). His resurrection marked the beginning of His **ultimate victory** over Satan.

Believers, through faith in **Jesus Christ**, are now invited to participate in His **kingdom** and live under His rule, despite the ongoing influence of the Devil in this world (2 Corinthians 4:4). Though Satan is referred to as the "prince of the power of the air" (Ephesians 2:2), Jesus has ultimate authority, and He calls His followers to **make disciples** of all nations, spreading the **good news** of salvation (Matthew 28:19-20).

We currently live in the **tension** between the fallen world influenced by the Devil and the spiritual **kingdom of God** established through Christ's victory. Believers are called to walk by faith, trusting in God's promises, and await the day when Jesus will return to **completely defeat Satan** and establish His eternal reign over a **restored creation** (Revelation 11:15). The **Book of Revelation** promises that God's dominion will be fully restored, and His people will reign with Him forever (Revelation 20-22).

This grand narrative of **creation**, **fall**, and **redemption** is a testament to God's **unwavering love, justice**, and **faithfulness**. Despite Adam and Eve's rebellion and the brokenness that followed, God's relentless pursuit of His people through **Jesus Christ** makes restoration possible. He offers **salvation** freely to all who believe, fulfilling His plan to bring His creation back under His rule. As believers, we are now called to live in light of this redemption, trusting in God's ultimate victory and sharing the message of His love and grace with the world.

Let me show you how this story affects us today. Every time you make a choice between good and evil, you're reliving a small part of what happened in that garden. And just like then, God still offers a way back to Him.

## Real Story Time

In the beginning, the earth was filled with peace, beauty, and purpose. God had given dominion—authority, control, stewardship, and responsibility—over the whole world to Adam, His beloved creation, intending for humanity to steward it with care and love. But in a moment of disobedience, Adam gave away that authority to the Devil. The Devil got Adam to give him dominion by deceiving Eve. Then, he tempted both her and Adam to disobey God's command. When they ate the forbidden fruit, they rebelled against God, and through that act of disobedience, they unknowingly handed over their God-given authority to the Devil, allowing him to take control over the earth.

Adam didn't realize the weight of his decision, but with it, sin and death entered the world, and the earth became a battleground. The Devil, filled with hatred for God, knew that his move would separate God from His greatest love, His people. This was why the Devil did it, aiming to hurt God by separating Him from those He cherished most. Despite the chaos, God's love for humanity never wavered. **God's greatest desire and love was to be with His people**, and the Devil sought to exploit this, knowing it would cause pain to God. But God, in His unfailing love for His people, would not abandon His creation to destruction.

Instead, God, motivated by His deep love for humanity, put together a plan to win back His beloved people. He quietly set in motion the most intricate and brilliant plan ever conceived—a plan of redemption that would free mankind from the Devil's grip and restore the broken relationship between God and His cherished creation.

God knew that His plan would need to be hidden from the Devil, so He began revealing pieces of it to chosen men and women throughout history. These revelations were written down, and over time, they became the Bible. In it, God planted over 300 prophecies, each one a clue to the coming of the Savior, but the full picture was shrouded in mystery. If the Devil knew what was coming, he would surely try to destroy it. But God, in His wisdom, allowed the Devil to believe he was winning.

As the world groaned under the weight of sin, God's love persisted. After the fall of Adam, humanity began to experience the consequences of sin—separation from God, physical death, and a corrupted world. Yet, God, in His mercy, provided a way for people to temporarily atone for their sins through animal sacrifices while waiting for God's master plan to come together. This system began after the first sin in the Garden of Eden, when God made garments of animal skins to cover Adam and Eve's shame, signifying the first shedding of blood to cover sin. This set the precedent that life must be sacrificed to atone for the wrongdoing of humanity.

As the years passed, God formalized the system of sacrifices in the law He gave to Moses. The blood of animals, though imperfect, temporarily covered the sins of His people. These sacrifices pointed back to the first death in Eden, and year after year, animals were offered as a payment for sin. This was the only way to maintain a relationship with God, who is perfect and cannot fellowship with sin. The Israelites, often struggling to grasp the full extent of God's plan, relied on these offerings to restore their connection with Him. However, the sacrifices could never fully remove sin, and its burden continued to weigh on the world.

Then, at the perfect moment, God sent His Son, Jesus, into the world. Jesus lived a sinless life, but the Devil, blinded by his own hatred, didn't see the plan unfolding before his eyes. All he saw was a chance to kill the Son of God, to claim victory over his greatest enemy. The Devil whispered into the hearts of men, stirring them to betray, arrest, and crucify Jesus. And on that dark day, when Jesus breathed His last breath on the cross, the Devil rejoiced, believing he had finally defeated God.

But what the Devil didn't realize was that he had played right into God's hands. The death of Jesus wasn't a defeat—it was the fulfillment of every prophecy, the breaking of every chain. In that moment, Jesus bore the sin of the world, fulfilling the law and providing a way for mankind to be restored to God. His sacrifice was the final and perfect atonement, replacing the old system of animal sacrifices, and His resurrection three days later was the ultimate victory, a declaration that death and sin no longer had the final say.

In the years that followed, God revealed the fullness of His plan through more writers, and the New Testament unveiled the hidden prophecies that had pointed to Jesus all along. Piece by piece, the story came together, showing the world that Jesus was the Redeemer, the one sent to rescue them from the Devil's dominion.

The Devil, realizing too late what had happened, was furious. But there was nothing he could do to undo what God had accomplished. The door to salvation had been opened, and anyone who believed in Jesus could walk through it, escaping the Devil's hold forever.

Yet, in His perfect justice, God did not force anyone to accept this salvation. It was a gift, offered freely to all who would believe. Those who recognized the truth and embraced God's love would find redemption, peace, and eternal life. The choice was theirs.

But now, knowing he had been defeated, the Devil shifted his strategy. He could no longer stop God's plan, but he could work to deceive as many of God's creations as possible, convincing them that the victory hadn't really been won. His new mission was to hide the blessings that came with God's kingdom, to blind people to the truth, and to keep them from entering into the life and freedom God offered.

The Devil became a master of lies, manipulating people's perceptions of love, joy, peace, and purpose. He twisted God's gifts, creating false versions to distract and deceive. He whispered lies into hearts, telling people that they could find contentment in power, wealth, or pleasure rather than in God's presence. He now lures people into bitterness, unforgiveness, and anger, knowing that these things will block them from experiencing God's peace.

He now takes something as pure as love between a man and a woman and distorts it into lust and self-serving relationships, convincing people that fleeting passion could fill the void only God's love could truly satisfy. The Devil crafts imitations of joy—promising happiness through materialism or temporary thrills—while hiding the deep, unshakable joy that comes from a life in God's kingdom.

He even attacks the peace God offers. Instead of trusting in God's plan, the Devil encourages people to seek peace through control, drugs, or false spirituality. He tempts them with shortcuts to achieve what only God can provide. The Devil has no original ideas, only perversions of what God has made good.

Through it all, the Devil's greatest lie is that there is a better way—his way—though it always leads to destruction. He manipulates hearts, offering the illusion of success while hiding the real blessings of walking in God's truth.

Yet, despite the Devil's efforts, God's love remains unwavering. He continues to reach out to His children, offering them the true gifts of His kingdom: love that is unconditional, peace that surpasses understanding, joy that overflows from His presence, and purpose that brings eternal meaning. God's plan is to rescue as many as possible, and the Devil's strategy is to stop them one by one—through deception, manipulation, and counterfeit promises.

The Devil knows his time is short, and his hatred for God fuels his relentless pursuit to lead people astray. But God's light continues to shine through, offering salvation, healing, and redemption to all who believe and walk into His kingdom. The battle rages on, but the victory is already won. God's people, armed with His truth and walking in His blessings, have everything they need to stand firm and live in the freedom He provides.

**The rest of the story** is that this will only play out for a little longer. We know that the battle with the Devil is already won and complete. Someday soon, Jesus will return. Now seated at the right hand of God in heaven, He will come back to collect all who believe in Him and send the Devil off to his eternal punishment. Sadly, all those whom the Devil has convinced to reject Jesus' gift of salvation will join him in eternal separation from God's love, joy, and peace.

But for those who have accepted Jesus, He will take them up to receive their eternal reward—life with Him forever in heaven. The Devil knows this is set in stone, and there is nothing he can do to stop it. Jesus, in His great love and patience, is holding off His return, giving as many people as possible the chance to accept His gift of salvation. He is waiting for more to choose Him, to walk away from the Devil's fake gifts, and to embrace the real life He offers.

Jesus will not force anyone to accept this gift, but He will continue to offer it to everyone, hoping that all will come to salvation, though some may still refuse. His love even extends to those who reject Him, so He delays His return, holding off as long as possible in His eternal plan. In the meantime, our role as believers is to walk in God's peace, joy, and love, sharing His kingdom with others. We are called to offer His gift of salvation to everyone we can. Yet, as we live in a world where the Devil still holds dominion, we must keep the full armor of God on, so we are not deceived or manipulated away from His kingdom. We must keep our eyes fixed on our eternal reward, knowing that one day soon, we will be with Him forever.

**In Conclusion**, In understanding the profound story of humanity's fall and redemption, we are reminded of God's unshakable love and His plan to restore the world through Christ. Living an unshakable life rooted in faith means recognizing that, despite the Devil's temporary influence, Christ's victory has already been secured. Aligning ourselves with God's true character helps us shed the misconceptions and myths that hinder our faith. It empowers us to face trials with unshakable confidence, knowing that redemption is not only promised but fulfilled through Jesus. Living abundantly in this truth allows us to fully trust in God's plan, walk in His dominion, and bring the light of His kingdom to a world in need. This is not just a call to endure but to thrive, as we confidently steward the life and authority God has restored to us through Christ.

## Dealing with Spiritual Conflict as Believers

Believers face a constant **spiritual conflict** between **God's kingdom** and the **Devil's influence**. Though the Devil was defeated through Jesus' death and resurrection (Colossians 2:15), his influence persists, and believers must navigate this conflict until God's ultimate rule is fully established. The Bible provides essential guidance for Christians to resist the Devil and live victoriously through faith in Jesus.

## The Devil is a Defeated Foe

Through Jesus' sacrifice, the Devil's power was broken. **Colossians 2:15** tells us that Christ "disarmed the powers and authorities," defeating the Devil through the cross. While the Devil continues to operate in the world, his ultimate defeat is assured, and believers stand in this victory.

## Believers' Authority Over the Devil

Believers are given **authority over the Devil** and demonic forces through their relationship with Christ. **Luke 10:19** says, "I have given you authority… to overcome all the power of the enemy." However, this authority comes not from themselves but through the **name of Jesus**. **Philippians 2:9-11** declares that every knee will bow to Jesus, and **Mark 16:17** affirms that in His name, believers can cast out demons. Believers must walk in step with the **Holy Spirit** to exercise this authority.

## Resisting the Devil and His Schemes

**James 4:7** instructs believers to submit to God and resist the Devil, causing him to flee. Recognizing and standing firm against the Devil's schemes, such as deception, temptation, and manipulation, is crucial (2 Corinthians 2:11). Much of the spiritual battle takes place in the **mind**, where the Devil plants doubt and lies. **2 Corinthians 10:4-5** teaches believers to take every thought captive and align it with Christ's truth.

## Stand Firm in Faith and Speak the Word of God

Believers are called to be **sober-minded and watchful** (1 Peter 5:8-9), standing firm in faith through prayer, worship, and obedience. The **Word of God** is a powerful weapon against the Devil's lies (Ephesians 6:17). When Jesus was tempted in the wilderness, He responded with Scripture (Matthew 4:1-11). Knowing and speaking God's Word is essential to defeating spiritual attacks.

## Walking in the Spirit and Putting on the Armor of God

Living by the **Holy Spirit** (Galatians 5:16) empowers believers to avoid the Devil's traps. **Ephesians 6:10-18** describes the **armor of God**, which protects believers from spiritual attacks:

- Belt of Truth: grounding in God's truth
- Breastplate of Righteousness: protection through Christ's righteousness
- Shoes of Peace: standing firm in the Gospel
- Shield of Faith: deflecting the enemy's attacks
- Helmet of Salvation: securing the mind in the hope of salvation
- Sword of the Spirit: wielding God's Word as a weapon
- Prayer: maintaining constant communication with God

## Submitting to God and Fleeing Temptation

To resist the Devil, believers must fully **submit to God's authority** (James 4:7) and rely on Him to **flee from temptation** (1 Corinthians

10:13). Trusting God's care and casting anxieties on Him (1 Peter 5:7) brings peace, protecting believers from the Devil's attacks. Using **spiritual weapons** like faith, righteousness, and truth (2 Corinthians 10:3-5) helps believers stand firm.

## Controlling Thoughts and Living in Victory

Romans 12:2 and Philippians 4:8 stress renewing the mind through God's Word. By focusing on what is true, noble, and pure, believers can transform their thinking and resist the enemy's attempts to plant negative thoughts. Thoughts shape behavior, so controlling them according to God's truth leads to victory.

Thoughts create emotions, emotions create behavior, and behavior creates the results in your life. So, whatever a person thinks about will result in what their life becomes. This is why it's vital to recognize the power of your thoughts and understand that they are the starting point for everything you experience. If your mind is filled with negative or self-defeating thoughts, it will lead to discouraging emotions, which shape harmful behaviors and, ultimately, undesired results. Therefore, it's crucial to be intentional about your thoughts and choose ones that align with the truth of how God sees you. Don't fall into the trap of listening to the enemy's lies and letting those thoughts define you. Instead, take every thought captive (2 Corinthians 10:5) and filter it through what you know God would want you to think about. By focusing on God's truth, you can create a life that reflects His purpose, peace, and abundance, living out the reality He has planned for you.

## The Rest of the Story: The Devil's Defeat and Jesus' Return

The Devil knows his defeat is inevitable, but he continues to deceive and lead people away from God's truth. He offers false versions of peace and success to keep people from living in God's true blessings. Yet, believers must recognize these lies and focus on Jesus, living in the reality of God's promises. **Revelation 11:15** tells us that one day,

Jesus will return to fully establish His kingdom, and the Devil will be eternally defeated. Until then, believers must walk in God's peace, wearing the full armor of God to avoid the enemy's traps.

## Conclusion

Believers are in a spiritual battle, but God has provided the tools and authority needed to walk in victory. Through **Jesus Christ**, believers have authority over the Devil, and by putting on the **Armor of God**, standing firm in **faith**, and walking in the **Holy Spirit**, they can overcome any attack. Living in alignment with God's truth and rejecting the Devil's lies leads to the **abundant life** that God desires for all His people.

## God's Victory Over the Enemy

Even though the enemy works tirelessly to pervert what God has created, we must remember that **God is sovereign**. The enemy may try to manipulate technology for his purposes, but **Jesus has already won the victory**. **Colossians 2:15** declares, *"And having disarmed the powers and authorities, he made a public spectacle of them, triumphing over them by the cross."* Satan's plans will ultimately fail, and God's purposes will prevail.

By understanding the enemy's strategies and **exposing** them to the light, we can walk in **victory** and use the gifts of **technology** as God intended—to **love**, to **serve**, to **bring the Gospel** to the ends of the earth, and to **advance His Kingdom**.

The key to defeating the enemy's strategies is to walk daily with the **Holy Spirit**, listening to His voice and following His lead. **Galatians 5:16** encourages us: *"So I say, walk by the Spirit, and you will not gratify the desires of the flesh."* When we walk in step with God's Spirit, we can use technology not for destruction, but for **God's glory**.

God's **master plan** for His people involves using every tool available to **bring salvation**, **freedom**, and **hope**. Through cloud computing,

AI, supercomputers, and other innovations, God is providing the Church with the ability to reach the nations and **transform lives**. And even though the enemy will try to stop us, we stand firm in the knowledge that God is with us, and His purposes will be fulfilled.

Let us be vigilant, wise, and discerning as we move forward, knowing that **God is in control** and that He will continue to use His people to bring about **His perfect plan**. **2 Corinthians 10:4-5** encourages us: *"The weapons we fight with are not the weapons of the world. On the contrary, they have divine power to demolish strongholds."* With God's power, we will overcome, and the enemy's schemes will be **exposed** and **defeated**.

# Chapter 11

## The Dark Side of the Internet

In this book, we explore how the spiritual battle described in Scripture extends into the digital age, where the internet has become a powerful tool for both good and evil. The enemy's tactics, which once thrived in the realms of human greed and selfishness during the Industrial Revolution, now infiltrate the vast and intricate web of the digital world, where everything from cloud-based computing to artificial intelligence plays a role. As Christians, we are called to not only be aware of these threats but also to protect ourselves spiritually and physically by putting on the full Armor of God.

### The Armor of God in Today's World

The Armor of God, as described in Ephesians 6:10-18, is just as relevant today as it was in the early church, perhaps even more so as the battlefield has shifted to new arenas, including the internet. Let's break down how each piece of this armor can be applied both spiritually and practically, especially in light of how technology is now being used to harm, deceive, and manipulate.

### Belt of Truth: Standing Against Digital Deception

The internet spreads lies fast. False stories go viral before the truth catches up. Scammers create fake websites that look real. The enemy loves this chaos, it makes truth harder to find. But God's truth cuts through every deception. Hackers thrive on deception, creating phishing schemes and scams that trick people into handing over sensitive information. This mirrors the spiritual attacks of the enemy, who seeks to lead us away from God's truth. The Belt of Truth keeps us as your inner lie detector. It helps you spot fake news, scams, and spiritual deception online.

Jesus said in John 14:6, "I am the way, the truth, and the life. No one comes to the Father except through me." As the internet fills our minds with distractions and lies, it is only through a firm foundation in the truth of God's Word that we can recognize the enemy's schemes. Just as we use strong security measures to protect our digital identities, we must be deeply rooted in the truth of Scripture to protect our spiritual identities.

## Breastplate of Righteousness: Guarding Our Hearts in a Corrupted World

In the digital world, hackers search for vulnerabilities in systems to exploit. Similarly, the devil seeks spiritual vulnerabilities—places where we are not living righteously—to infiltrate and corrupt us. The **Breastplate of Righteousness** protects our hearts from being corrupted by the temptations and sins that abound on the internet.

Proverbs 4:23 says, "Above all else, guard your heart, for everything you do flows from it." The enemy uses internet-based temptations, such as pornography, gossip, and envy on social media, to corrupt our hearts and lead us into sin. But living a life of righteousness acts as a barrier against these attacks, just as strong cybersecurity measures protect our digital systems from breaches.

## Shield of Faith: Defending Against Digital Attacks

Faith is our defense against the spiritual attacks of the enemy, just as antivirus software and firewalls are defenses against digital viruses and malware. The **Shield of Faith** is meant to protect us from the fiery arrows of doubt, fear, and temptation that Satan sends our way.

Ephesians 6:16 tells us, "In all circumstances take up the shield of faith, with which you can extinguish all the flaming darts of the evil one." Today, those darts can come through screens—doubts stirred by harmful messages, fear propagated by disturbing content, and temptations luring us into sin. Faith in God's promises deflects these attacks, much like cybersecurity measures defend our systems from hackers.

## Helmet of Salvation: Protecting Our Minds from Confusion

Hackers often aim to confuse and manipulate. Similarly, Satan seeks to confuse our minds with doubt about our salvation, trying to make us question who we are in Christ. The **Helmet of Salvation** protects our minds from the spiritual confusion and attacks that come through the distractions and influences of the internet.

In a world where so much content seeks to sway our thinking—be it through news, social media, or advertising—the assurance of salvation guards our minds. Colossians 3:2 says, "Set your minds on things above, not on earthly things." With the internet bombarding us with information that often pulls us away from eternal truths, the Helmet of Salvation helps us remain focused on God's plan for our lives.

## Sword of the Spirit: Combatting Digital and Spiritual Lies

The **Sword of the Spirit**, which is the Word of God, is our offensive weapon in both the spiritual and digital battles we face. Jesus used Scripture to defeat Satan's temptations in the wilderness, and we must use it to combat the lies and distractions that we encounter on the internet.

Hebrews 4:12 tells us, "For the word of God is alive and active, sharper than any double-edged sword." In today's context, this means using Scripture to discern truth from the lies we encounter online—whether they are false doctrines, manipulative content, or harmful ideologies. Just as a hacker uses malicious code to corrupt, we use the Word of God to expose and destroy the lies of the enemy.

# The Enemy's Tactics in the Digital World

The enemy's tactics in the digital world are pervasive and deeply rooted in the same destructive desires that have been present throughout human history—greed, selfishness, and deception. Just as greed and exploitation were central to the Industrial Revolution, where the pursuit of wealth and power often came at the expense of people's well-being, Satan is now leveraging the internet as a tool to exploit our vulnerabilities, distract us from God's purpose, and lead us into spiritual and even physical destruction.

## How Satan Uses Hackers and Cyber Crime

Hackers are among the most prominent tools in Satan's digital arsenal. Just as the enemy deceives and manipulates to break into our spiritual lives, hackers break into systems with the intent to steal, destroy, and cause chaos. Their motivations—whether greed, pride, or simply the thrill of causing harm—reflect the devil's own goals.

## Theft and Identity Fraud

John 10:10 tells us, "The thief comes only to steal and kill and destroy." This verse reveals Satan's desire to steal what God has given us, kill our joy, and destroy our faith. Similarly, hackers steal personal information, financial data, and even intellectual property, causing severe damage to the lives of their victims.

Identity theft, one of the most prevalent cyber crimes today, mirrors Satan's tactic of trying to steal our spiritual identity. When hackers steal someone's identity, they cause confusion, financial loss, and emotional turmoil. In the same way, Satan tries to make us forget our true identity in Christ. He wants to lead us into insecurity, confusion, and fear, so we forget that we are children of God, protected and saved by His grace.

# Ransomware and Spiritual Paralysis

Ransomware is another cybercrime that reflects Satan's spiritual attacks. Hackers use this malicious software to lock users out of their own systems, demanding ransom in exchange for restoring access. In a spiritual sense, Satan tries to paralyze believers by holding them hostage to sin, guilt, shame, or fear, making them feel as though they need to "pay" something to be free.

But Scripture tells us that Christ has already paid the ransom for us. Ephesians 1:7 says, "In Him, we have redemption through His blood, the forgiveness of sins, in accordance with the riches of God's grace." Satan's attempts to ransom our souls through guilt and shame are lies. Just as we should never pay the ransom to hackers, we should never fall for the enemy's deceitful claims that we are unworthy of God's love or forgiveness.

# Immoral Content: A Gateway to Sin

One of the most visible ways the enemy uses the internet to lead people astray is through immoral content. Pornography, violent media, and sites that promote hatred or division are rampant online, and they are designed to appeal to the basest human instincts. These forms of content trap people in cycles of addiction, shame, and spiritual bondage.

# Pornography and the Destruction of Purity

One of the most significant issues online is the prevalence of pornography, which Satan uses to destroy purity and distort God's design for intimacy. 1 Corinthians 6:18 says, "Flee from sexual immorality. All other sins a person commits are outside the body, but whoever sins sexually, sins against their own body." Pornography is not just a physical sin; it is a spiritual trap that distorts the mind and the soul. It feeds lust, which leads to isolation, shame, and ultimately a fractured relationship with God.

The internet has made this sin easily accessible, and Satan uses it to destroy marriages, families, and individual lives. What's worse, this content often escalates, pulling people deeper into more damaging material. Like malware that infiltrates a computer system, corrupting everything it touches, pornography corrupts the mind and heart, making it increasingly difficult to walk in righteousness.

## Violence and Hatred Online

In addition to sexual immorality, the internet is filled with content that glorifies violence, hatred, and division. News outlets, social media platforms, and entertainment often spread messages of anger and conflict, feeding the enemy's goal of division and chaos. Proverbs 6:16-19 warns that God hates those who stir up dissension among brothers. Yet, on the internet, this behavior is often rewarded with attention, likes, and shares.

Satan uses this content to desensitize people to the value of human life and to stir up anger, bitterness, and strife. By filling our hearts with hatred, the enemy makes it difficult for us to walk in love and unity as Christ commanded. Ephesians 4:31-32 instructs, "Let all bitterness and wrath and anger and clamor and slander be put away from you, along with all malice. Be kind to one another, tenderhearted, forgiving one another, as God in Christ forgave you." Yet, the internet often encourages the opposite, pulling us into a world of constant conflict and division.

## Misinformation and False Teachings

The internet is also a breeding ground for misinformation and false teachings. Satan, the "father of lies" (John 8:44), uses these tools to lead people away from biblical truth. Whether it's through the spread of conspiracy theories, distortions of the gospel, or outright heresies, the enemy uses digital platforms to confuse believers and non-believers alike.

# Conspiracy Theories and Spiritual Distrust

In recent years, conspiracy theories have spread like wildfire across the internet, feeding fear, distrust, and paranoia. These theories often distract people from focusing on God and His Word, leading them to place their faith in worldly "truths" rather than eternal truths. 2 Timothy 4:3-4 warns, "For the time will come when people will not put up with sound doctrine. Instead, to suit their own desires, they will gather around them a great number of teachers to say what their itching ears want to hear. They will turn their ears away from the truth and turn aside to myths."

Satan uses these myths and conspiracies to keep people in a state of fear and uncertainty, pulling them away from a reliance on God. When people become obsessed with hidden worldly agendas, they lose sight of the true spiritual battle being waged and the peace that comes from trusting in God's sovereignty.

# Heresies and Doctrinal Errors

False teachings and heresies are nothing new, but the internet has amplified their reach. Today, anyone can claim to be a teacher or preacher, regardless of their qualifications or spiritual understanding. As a result, many believers are led astray by teachings that sound appealing but are not grounded in Scripture.

Jesus warned about this in Matthew 7:15, saying, "Beware of false prophets, who come to you in sheep's clothing but inwardly are ravenous wolves." These false teachers prey on people's desires for success, wealth, or comfort, offering a distorted gospel that is far removed from the truth of God's Word. The prosperity gospel, for example, is often spread online, promising financial blessing and health in exchange for faith, but ignoring the Bible's teachings on suffering, sacrifice, and humility.

The spread of false doctrine online requires believers to be more discerning than ever. We are called to "test the spirits" (1 John 4:1)

164

and ensure that what we are consuming is truly from God. This requires a deep knowledge of Scripture, a commitment to prayer, and the guidance of the Holy Spirit.

# Time-Wasting and Distractions: A Strategy for Mediocrity

Satan's digital strategies are not always overtly evil; many are far more subtle. One of the most effective ways the enemy uses the internet is through time-wasting distractions. Social media, video games, endless newsfeeds, and entertainment platforms are designed to keep us scrolling, watching, and clicking for hours. What seems like harmless fun can quickly become a black hole of wasted time.

## The Danger of Complacency

Ephesians 5:15-16 urges us, "Look carefully then how you walk, not as unwise but as wise, making the best use of the time, because the days are evil." The enemy knows that if he can keep us distracted, he can prevent us from fulfilling God's purpose for our lives. We may not be committing obvious sins, but by allowing ourselves to be lulled into complacency and mediocrity, we are missing out on the calling God has placed on us.

The internet is designed to keep us entertained and engaged, often at the expense of our spiritual growth. Satan uses this constant engagement to steal our time—time that could be spent in prayer, reading Scripture, serving others, or growing in our faith. When we are consumed by digital distractions, we are not alert to the spiritual battle around us, and the enemy gains ground.

## Vigilance in the Digital Age

In the same way that Satan used greed and selfishness during the Industrial Revolution to exploit and destroy God's creation, he is now using the internet to wage war against God's people. Hackers, immoral content, false teachings, and time-wasting distractions are just some of the tactics the enemy employs to lead us away from God's purpose for our lives.

But as Christians, we are not without defense. By putting on the Armor of God (Ephesians 6:10-18), staying grounded in Scripture, and being vigilant in our digital lives, we can resist the enemy's attacks and stand firm in our faith. The internet can be a tool for great good or great evil, and it is up to us to use it wisely, ensuring that our time, attention, and hearts remain focused on God. As James 4:7 reminds us, "Submit yourselves, then, to God. Resist the devil, and he will flee from you." In both the digital and spiritual realms, this is our ultimate strategy for victory.

## Cloud Computing and the Enemy's Influence

Think of cloud computing like a giant digital storage unit. While it lets us access our files from anywhere, it can also leave our personal information vulnerable to hackers.. Spiritually, Satan uses the "cloud" of the digital world to spread confusion and destruction. Much like how hackers seek to access personal data stored in the cloud, the devil seeks to access our thoughts and influence our minds by bombarding us with worldly distractions.

However, cloud computing can also be used for good. Just as God gives us the ability to use technology for productivity and the spread of His Word, the enemy tries to corrupt that potential for evil. We must be vigilant in how we use these technologies, remembering that they can either serve God's kingdom or become tools in the enemy's hands.

## Artificial Intelligence and Spiritual Deception

Artificial intelligence (AI) has incredible potential for both good and evil. AI can help us make better decisions, automate processes, and even enhance our relationship with God by giving us tools to study His Word. However, the enemy also uses AI to manipulate and deceive. AI algorithms are often designed to maximize engagement by showing us content that fuels our biases, feeds our desires, or manipulates our emotions.

Satan uses this aspect of AI to keep people trapped in echo chambers where they only see content that reinforces sinful behaviors, false beliefs, or destructive ideologies. Romans 12:2 warns us, "Do not conform to the pattern of this world, but be transformed by the renewing of your mind." As AI increasingly shapes our digital experiences, we must be discerning and allow the Holy Spirit to renew our minds, so we are not conformed to worldly patterns.

## Software, Malware, and Spiritual Attacks

Just as hackers use malicious software (malware) to infiltrate and corrupt computer systems, Satan uses "spiritual malware" to corrupt our hearts and minds. This spiritual malware can take the form of lies, temptations, and distractions that seem harmless at first but slowly erode our relationship with God.

James 1:14-15 explains how temptation works, saying, "But each person is tempted when they are dragged away by their own evil desire and enticed. Then, after desire has conceived, it gives birth to sin; and sin, when it is full-grown, gives birth to death." Just as a computer can be destroyed by malware if left unchecked, our spiritual lives can be destroyed if we allow sin to take root.

## The Spiritual-Physical Connection in the Digital Age

The digital world is not separate from the spiritual realm; the two are deeply intertwined. The internet, artificial intelligence, and cloud computing are all part of God's creation, just as the physical world is. However, just as Satan used the greed of the Industrial Revolution to harm people and twist God's creation, he now uses the internet to lead people away from God's plan.

Isaiah 5:20 warns us, "Woe to those who call evil good and good evil, who put darkness for light and light for darkness." The enemy is actively working to distort God's creation—the internet included—using it for destruction rather than for good. But as believers, we are called to redeem these tools, using them to spread the gospel, build God's kingdom, and protect ourselves and others from the enemy's schemes.

## Practical Steps for Digital and Spiritual Protection

In today's world, spiritual and practical protection go hand in hand. Just as we take steps to secure our computers with firewalls, antivirus software, and strong passwords, we must take spiritual steps to protect ourselves from the enemy's attacks.

1. **Prayer**: Stay connected to God through prayer, asking for wisdom and protection. James 1:5 reminds us, "If any of you lacks wisdom, you should ask God, who gives generously to all without finding fault, and it will be given to you."
2. **Scripture**: Study God's Word regularly so you can discern truth from lies. Psalm 119:105 says, "Your word is a lamp for my feet, a light on my path." Being rooted in Scripture helps us navigate the complex digital landscape.
3. **Accountability**: Surround yourself with godly people who will encourage you to stay on the path of righteousness. Hebrews 10:24-25 encourages us to "spur one another on toward love and good deeds, not giving up meeting together, as some are in the habit of doing, but encouraging one another."
4. **Discernment in Technology Use**: Be intentional about how you use technology. Don't allow it to become a tool for the enemy to distract or deceive you. Instead, use it to further God's purposes, knowing that every click, every post, and every decision online is part of a larger spiritual battle.

# Victory in Christ

Despite the enemy's attempts to use technology for evil, we are assured of victory in Christ. James 4:7 promises us, "Submit yourselves, then, to God. Resist the devil, and he will flee from you." By putting on the Armor of God, remaining vigilant, and using technology for good, we can resist the enemy's strategies and stand firm in our faith.

The digital world may be a battlefield, but we are not alone in this fight. God equips us with everything we need to stand strong, and through His power, we can overcome the enemy's schemes—both spiritual and digital—living lives that are victorious and aligned with His will.

# Conclusion for Part 3: Technology—The Battleground Between Good and Evil

As we conclude Part 3, it becomes undeniably clear that the digital age, while full of technological wonders, is also a battleground where God's kingdom collides with the enemy's schemes. Like the Industrial Revolution before it, this era of innovation, defined by artificial intelligence, cloud computing, and advanced networks, presents us with unparalleled opportunities to do good and spread the Gospel, yet also contains significant dangers when misused by the enemy. We find ourselves standing at the crossroads of immense potential and unprecedented threats.

In the same way that believers fought against the corruption and exploitation of the Industrial Revolution, we are called to rise today and reclaim technology for God's kingdom. Whether we harness AI to share the Gospel in unreached nations, use cloud platforms to spread God's Word in every language, or develop digital tools to minister to the lost and hurting, we are part of a divine plan that seeks to advance His kingdom on Earth.

But we must be vigilant, for the enemy's tactics are subtle and deceptive. He uses the very tools God has blessed us with—technology, creativity, innovation—to distract, deceive, and destroy. He sows seeds of division through social media, manipulates minds with misinformation, and draws people into destructive digital addictions. This spiritual battle is real, and as believers, we are called to put on the full armor of God and fight back.

Let's be inspired by stories of great men and women of faith who have stood against evil, like William Wilberforce, who fought to abolish slavery, and Elizabeth Fry, who worked to reform prisons. Their battles were fierce, but they never wavered because they walked step by step with God. Today, we face new battles—battles that unfold in the invisible realm of cyberspace, but battles, nonetheless. And just as those who came before us stood firm, we must take our place on the frontlines of the digital world, equipped with God's wisdom and power.

In the story of Thomas, we see the life-changing impact of fully committing to the spiritual armor God provides. Thomas learned that half measures weren't enough to withstand the enemy's attacks—only by embracing the full armor, trusting God's guidance, and using Scripture as his weapon was he able to see transformation in his life. This story reminds us that no matter how overwhelming the enemy's influence in technology may seem, we too can experience victory when we walk in faith, armed with the truth of God's Word.

**Call to Action: Moving Forward in Spiritual and Digital Victory**

As we prepare to dive into the next section, let this be your charge: Do not shy away from the battle, and do not underestimate the power of God to redeem what the enemy has corrupted. You are part of God's army, equipped with spiritual weapons that can destroy the strongholds of the enemy, both in your personal life and in the digital world around you. Take the next step in your journey with confidence, knowing that God is with you, guiding your every move.

Let us walk together, step by step, with the Holy Spirit as our guide, using technology not for destruction but to build, redeem, and advance God's kingdom. Be bold in your pursuit of truth, diligent in prayer, and unwavering in your trust in God's ultimate victory. The enemy may prowl like a roaring lion, seeking to devour, but with God on our side, we stand firm, knowing that the battle is already won.

Now, go forward and continue your reading—step into the next part with an open heart, ready to uncover even deeper truths about the spiritual warfare we face and the ways in which we, as God's people, can take a stand against the enemy's schemes. Together, we will walk in victory, reclaiming technology for God's glory and advancing His purposes in this digital age.

With every click, every decision, and every prayer, you are making an impact for eternity. Stay strong, stay grounded in God's Word, and be ready to continue this incredible journey of faith. The best is yet to come!

# Part 4

# Practical Steps of physical protection

Unshakable Digital Defense: God's Blueprint for Physical and Spiritual Protection in a Technological World"

"Securing Our Lives and Faith in the Digital Age with God's Wisdom and Modern Cybersecurity"

In Part 4, *"Practical Steps of Physical Protection: Unshakable Digital Defense,"* we explore how God's wisdom intersects with modern cybersecurity to provide a blueprint for protecting both our spiritual and physical lives in the digital age. As technology continues to evolve, the threats we face become more complex, but so do the tools we have at our disposal to combat them. This section will walk you through practical strategies to secure your personal, family, and business digital spaces, ensuring that we remain vigilant stewards of what God has entrusted to us. By embracing modern cybersecurity tools—just as we arm ourselves with spiritual defenses—we can navigate today's technological landscape with confidence and faith, knowing that God provides both the wisdom and the means to keep us safe.

# Chapter 12

## Gods Physical Protection

In the digital age, the internet has become a powerful tool that can be used both for good and for evil. The Industrial Revolution brought both progress and problems. Similarly, today's technology opens doors for both good and evil. We find ourselves at a crossroads where we must choose how we engage with the internet, artificial intelligence (AI), cloud-based software, apps, and other digital tools.

This intersection of technology and faith reveals a critical truth: God has always called His people to be vigilant, both spiritually and physically. As Christians, we must not only equip ourselves with the Armor of God but also with practical tools to protect ourselves, our families, and our communities from the enemy's digital strategies. One of the most powerful ways to do this is through proper cybersecurity. Just as God raised heroes in the Industrial Revolution to save workers and protect His creation, He is raising new digital heroes—cybersecurity experts and developers—who can help protect His people and redeem His creation in the online world.

## The Role of Cybersecurity in God's Covenant and Abundant Life

God's covenant with His people has always been about providing safety, protection, and abundance. Deuteronomy 28:12 tells us, "The Lord will open the heavens, the storehouse of His bounty, to send rain on your land in season and to bless all the work of your hands." Just as God desires to bless the work of our hands in the physical realm, He also wants to bless and protect the work of our hands in the digital realm. Cybersecurity is one of the modern tools God can use to ensure His people remain safe and prosperous in this interconnected world.

Cybersecurity serves as a defense against the enemy's attacks in the same way that the Armor of God shields us from spiritual attacks. By putting proper safeguards in place, we can ensure that we are not only protected physically from cyber threats but also that our spiritual mission remains uncompromised. In fact, cyber defense and spiritual defense are deeply intertwined, as both require vigilance, discernment, and preparation.

# The Importance of Proper Password Management

One of the most critical aspects of cybersecurity is managing and using passwords correctly. With the complexity of modern passwords, it's easy to become frustrated and fall into bad habits, like using the same password for everything or writing them down on sticky notes. While these shortcuts may seem convenient, they leave your personal and business information highly vulnerable to cyberattacks. Let's explore why password management is so important and how we can make it easier.

## Why Good Password Management Matters
Passwords serve as the first line of defense in protecting your accounts and sensitive data. When passwords are weak or reused across different platforms, you're at a much greater risk of hacking, identity theft, and data breaches. Creating strong, unique passwords for each account and regularly updating them helps reduce these risks and enhances your security.

## Common Password Mistakes

Many people make simple but dangerous mistakes when managing their passwords:

- **Reusing passwords across multiple accounts**: If one account is breached, all linked accounts are at risk.

- **Using weak passwords**: Short or predictable passwords can easily be cracked by automated tools.
- **Failure to update passwords**: Stale passwords leave accounts open to exploitation over time.
- **Ignoring two-factor authentication (2FA)**: Not using 2FA eliminates an extra layer of security that can prevent unauthorized access.
- **Storing passwords insecurely**: Keeping passwords on sticky notes or in unencrypted files invites theft.

**Vulnerabilities From Poor Practices** Poor password habits create significant vulnerabilities. **Brute force attacks** target weak or common passwords, while **credential stuffing** exploits reused passwords across multiple sites. Additionally, you may fall victim to **phishing** attacks, where hackers trick you into revealing your passwords by pretending to be legitimate services.

**Effective Password Management Tools** To improve your security, using password management tools can help. These tools securely store your passwords and even generate strong, unique ones for you. Consider using trusted options such as:

- LastPass, 1Password, Dashlane, Bitwarden, Keeper Security

These tools make managing passwords easier and more secure, removing the need to remember every password while ensuring your accounts are well-protected.

## A Biblical Perspective on Password Management

From a biblical standpoint, password management aligns with the principles of wisdom, stewardship, and integrity. Proverbs 27:12 tells us that "the prudent see danger and take refuge," encouraging us to take precautions to protect ourselves. Nehemiah 4:9 shows that while we trust God for protection, we must also take practical steps, much like using a password manager to protect our digital assets. Proverbs

10:9 reminds us to walk in integrity, which includes responsibly managing what has been entrusted to us.

Password management may seem like a small task, but it's vital for keeping your digital life safe. By avoiding common mistakes and using password management tools, you protect your information and follow biblical principles of wisdom, stewardship, and integrity. Making simple changes to your password habits can lead to better security and peace of mind in an increasingly digital world.

# The Importance of Cybersecurity in the Digital Age

Just as God has equipped us with the spiritual tools to fight against the enemy, He has also provided us with the intellectual capabilities and technological tools to defend ourselves in the digital world. The internet, apps, AI, cloud-based computing, and computer-based software all require cybersecurity because, without protection, these technologies become vulnerable to attacks. These attacks are not just technical or financial—they can also have spiritual consequences. A hacked system can result in lost opportunities for ministry, disruption of important work, or even the theft of personal identity, which can lead to spiritual discouragement and confusion.

### 1. The Internet: A Gateway for Both Good and Evil

The internet is the highway on which most digital activity occurs. It is a powerful tool for spreading the gospel, building community, and enabling business. However, it is also a primary target for cyberattacks. Hackers, motivated by greed, pride, or the thrill of chaos, often attack systems with the intent to steal data, disrupt operations, or spread malicious content.

God can use cybersecurity to protect His people in these digital spaces, ensuring that the internet remains a tool for His glory. For example, firewalls and Virtual Private Networks (VPNs) serve as critical defenses. A firewall acts as a barrier between a trusted internal network and untrusted external networks (like the internet), allowing only safe, authorized data to pass through. Similarly, VPNs encrypt your internet connection, making it difficult for hackers to intercept sensitive information.

# How VPNs Work

A VPN (Virtual Private Network) works by creating an encrypted tunnel between your device and the internet. When you use public WiFi without a VPN, it's like having a conversation that anyone can overhear. With a VPN, it's like whispering in a secret code that only you and your intended recipient can understand. This ensures that all the data passing between you and the websites you visit is protected from prying eyes. VPNs are particularly useful when using public Wi-Fi, as unsecured networks are prime targets for hackers. Without a VPN, sensitive data such as passwords, credit card details, or personal emails could be intercepted and stolen. With a VPN, your connection is encrypted, ensuring that even if a hacker tries to intercept your data, they can't read it.

Proverbs 4:23 tells us, "Above all else, guard your heart, for everything you do flows from it." In the same way, we must guard our digital lives because so much of our modern work and ministry flows through the internet. Just as the Belt of Truth keeps us centered on God's truth in the spiritual realm, these digital tools keep our internet connections secure and protected from the enemy's deception.

## 2. Computer-Based Software: Protecting Our Devices from Malware and Viruses

Computer-based software is another critical area that needs cybersecurity. Malware, viruses, ransomware, spyware, and other malicious programs can target computers, steal data, damage files, or lock users out of their systems. Without protection, these malicious programs can wreak havoc on personal, professional, and ministry-related work.

**Types of Malware and Viruses:**

- **Viruses**: These malicious programs attach themselves to legitimate files and spread to other files or systems when opened. Viruses can corrupt or delete data, and they often slow down a system significantly. Much like spiritual attacks, viruses may remain dormant until triggered, causing damage when least expected.
- **Trojans**: A Trojan is a type of malware disguised as legitimate software. Once installed, it can provide unauthorized access to your system, allowing hackers to steal sensitive data or install further malicious software. This is much like false teachers in the spiritual realm who appear to be trustworthy but have harmful intentions.
- **Keyloggers**: Keyloggers are a type of spyware that records every keystroke you make, often used by hackers to steal passwords and sensitive information. This mirrors the enemy's tactic of watching for weak moments, ready to strike when we least expect it.
- **Ransomware**: Ransomware encrypts your files and demands payment in exchange for the decryption key. It is similar to how Satan seeks to hold people hostage to sin, guilt, or fear, paralyzing them spiritually and preventing them from moving forward.
- **Spyware**: Spyware is used to gather information about a person's online activities without their knowledge. It monitors browsing habits, login credentials, and more, often with the intent of selling the data or using it for further attacks. This can be compared to the enemy's method of subtly observing our weaknesses to exploit them later.

**How They Get In:**

Malware and viruses often enter systems through infected email attachments, malicious websites, or software downloads from untrusted sources. Phishing scams, where users are tricked into clicking on a harmful link or downloading malicious content, are common avenues for infection.

**How to Protect Against Malware and Viruses:**

Antivirus software is essential for detecting and removing these threats before they cause significant damage. Modern antivirus programs provide real-time protection by scanning files and programs as they are opened or downloaded. This constant vigilance mirrors how we are to "pray without ceasing" (1 Thessalonians 5:17), always alert to spiritual dangers.

Firewalls add another layer of protection, monitoring incoming and outgoing traffic and blocking any suspicious activity. This is akin to spiritual discernment, where we guard our hearts and minds against the enemy's attempts to infiltrate our thoughts and actions.

### 3. Cloud-Based Software: Securing Our Data in the Cloud

Cloud storage is like having a secure digital storage unit you can access from anywhere. Instead of keeping files just on your computer, you store them online where they're protected but always available. However, the cloud is also a prime target for hackers, who can exploit vulnerabilities to steal sensitive information. This is particularly dangerous for businesses and ministries that store large amounts of personal or financial data.

Encryption is one of the most important tools for securing data in the cloud. Encryption scrambles data, making it unreadable to anyone without the proper decryption key. This is much like how the Holy Spirit "seals" us for salvation, making us secure in Christ. Ephesians 1:13 says, "When you believed, you were marked in him with a seal, the promised Holy Spirit." Just as encryption ensures that our data is safe, the Holy Spirit guarantees our security in God's kingdom.

Multi-factor authentication (MFA) is another key tool for cloud security. MFA requires multiple forms of verification before granting access, ensuring that even if a hacker steals a password, they cannot access the system without an additional authentication factor. This mirrors the spiritual principle of accountability, where multiple layers of support and discernment help protect us from falling into temptation. Proverbs 27:17 tells us, "As iron sharpens iron, so one person sharpens another." Just as we rely on others to help us stay strong in faith, multi-factor authentication adds extra layers of protection for our digital lives.

## 4. Apps and Mobile Devices: Securing Our Daily Tools

Mobile apps and devices are an integral part of daily life, and they are also vulnerable to cyberattacks. Malicious apps, insecure connections, and unpatched software can leave mobile devices open to exploitation.

Mobile device management (MDM) software allows organizations and individuals to monitor, manage, and secure mobile devices. This is similar to the role of a shepherd, who watches over and protects the flock from danger. Psalm 23:1 reminds us, "The Lord is my shepherd, I shall not want." Just as the Lord watches over us, MDM software helps watch over and protect mobile devices from harm.

Additionally, users should be wary of downloading apps from untrusted sources. Many malicious apps masquerade as useful tools but instead install malware or steal personal information. This is much like the false teachers that the Bible warns us about in 2 Peter 2:1: "But there were also false prophets among the people, just as there will be false teachers among you. They will secretly introduce destructive heresies, even denying the sovereign Lord who bought them." In both cases, discernment is key to avoiding danger.

## 5. Artificial Intelligence (AI): Potential and Danger

AI has incredible potential for good, from improving healthcare to enhancing productivity. However, it also has the potential for harm if misused. AI algorithms, especially those used in social media and advertising, can manipulate emotions, fuel addictions, and reinforce harmful behaviors.

AI-driven cyberattacks, such as automated phishing schemes and advanced hacking techniques, are becoming more sophisticated. Cybersecurity experts are now using AI to combat these threats by developing AI-driven security systems that can identify and respond to attacks in real-time. This is akin to how God uses spiritual gifts to protect His people and build His kingdom. 1 Corinthians 12:7 says, "Now to each one the manifestation of the Spirit is given for the common good." Just as AI can be used to protect systems, the Holy Spirit equips believers with gifts that help us protect and edify one another.

It's important to approach AI with both caution and discernment. While it can be a powerful tool for good, it can also be used to exploit, manipulate, and deceive. Proverbs 3:5-6 tells us, "Trust in the Lord with all your heart and lean not on your own understanding; in all your ways submit to him, and he will make your paths straight." This is a reminder that while AI can enhance our lives, our ultimate trust must remain in the Lord, not in human inventions.

### 6. Networks: The Backbone of Digital Communication

A network is a collection of computers, servers, and other devices connected to share resources and information. Networks allow for the sharing of data, but they are also vulnerable to cyberattacks. Hackers often exploit vulnerabilities in networks to gain unauthorized access, steal data, or disrupt operations.

To protect networks, several cybersecurity measures can be implemented:

- **Firewalls**: Firewalls control the flow of data between networks, blocking unauthorized access and protecting against cyber threats.
- **Intrusion Detection Systems (IDS)**: IDS monitors network traffic for suspicious activity and alerts administrators to potential attacks.
- **Network Encryption**: Encrypting data as it travels across a network ensures that even if a hacker intercepts the data, they cannot read it.

These tools are much like the spiritual defenses we build to protect our communities and families. Just as networks need constant monitoring and protection, our spiritual lives need ongoing vigilance to guard against the enemy's attacks.

## Cybersecurity as a Spiritual Defense

Cybersecurity not only protects us physically by securing our devices and data, but it also has spiritual implications. Just as we need strong passwords and firewalls to protect our systems from hackers, we need strong spiritual defenses to protect our hearts and minds from the enemy's attacks. God works in partnership with His people, using both spiritual and practical tools to protect us and ensure that we live abundant lives.

Throughout history, God has raised up heroes to protect and save His creation. During the Industrial Revolution, there were individuals who fought against the exploitation of workers, ensuring their safety and dignity. Today, God is raising up digital heroes—cybersecurity experts, developers, and even everyday people—who will protect His people in the online world. These individuals are not only keeping us safe from cyber threats but are also helping to redeem God's creation by ensuring that technology is used for good, not evil.

Just as Nehemiah led the Israelites in rebuilding the walls of Jerusalem for protection, God is calling us to build strong digital walls—cyber defenses—that will protect us from the enemy's attacks. Nehemiah 4:14 says, "Don't be afraid of them. Remember the Lord, who is great and awesome, and fight for your families, your sons, and your daughters, your wives, and your homes." In the same way, we must not be afraid of the enemy's digital attacks. Instead, we must remember that God is with us, and we must fight—both spiritually and practically—to protect what God has entrusted to us.

# Partnering with God in the Digital World

Cybersecurity is not just a technical necessity; it is a spiritual tool that God can use to protect His people and further His covenant. As we engage in the digital world, we must be vigilant, discerning, and prepared. By putting on the Armor of God and employing proper cybersecurity measures, we can protect ourselves from the enemy's attacks and ensure that we are using technology for God's glory.

God desires for His people to live abundant lives, and this includes being safe and secure in both the physical and digital realms. John 10:10 tells us, "The thief comes only to steal and kill and destroy; I have come that they may have life, and have it to the full." By partnering with God, using the tools He has provided, and remaining vigilant in our spiritual and practical defenses, we can live that abundant life—protected, empowered, and fully aligned with His will.

# Chapter 13

## My Story of Technology

I understand where you're coming from. Many of us, myself included, have lived through a time when the world was far less digitally connected. I grew up in a generation that didn't have computers, smartphones, or the internet, and yet here we are today, living in a world where technology is embedded in almost every aspect of our lives. We've seen a massive transformation. Paper calendars became online tools. Handwritten notes turned into emails and texts. And let me be the first to say that this journey into the digital age hasn't always been smooth or enjoyable. But I've realized something important: Change, though uncomfortable, can also be a tool for God's blessings.

One of my first business mentors often told me, "The only thing we can really count on in this world is change, and we must always be prepared for it." While I now realize we can count on much more than just change, it's still a good reminder that everything around us is constantly shifting. Let's stay flexible and adapt as things change.

## Understanding the Role of Technology in God's Plan

As you can probably tell, I don't like change, especially when it's thrust upon me without my say. But I've come to recognize that God works through all things—even the things that make us uneasy. There was a time when I moved from using a paper calendar to an online calendar, a time when I transitioned from having phone calls recorded on pink slips to voicemail. I didn't ask for those changes, and at first, I resisted. But over time, God showed me that embracing those tools didn't mean I was giving in to something negative—it meant I was stepping into a place where God could continue to work through me in new and powerful ways.

In Ecclesiastes 3:1, we are reminded, *"There is a time for everything and a season for every activity under the heavens."* The world is constantly changing, and that includes the tools we use. But God remains constant, and if we align ourselves with Him, we can learn to discern which changes He is calling us to embrace for His glory.

## Learning to Adapt: From Resistance to Revelation

As someone who started my career in the financial sector, running an investment management company, I've seen firsthand how technology can completely shift the way we operate. I moved from making decisions based on knowledge that I read about or experienced, to using software that spit out data to guide my decisions. At first, I had no desire to use these tools—I wanted to stick with what I knew. But slowly, I began to see the hand of God in this transformation. Proverbs 4:7 says, *"The beginning of wisdom is this: Get wisdom. Though it costs all you have, get understanding."*

I could have chosen to stay with the old ways—the comfortable ways. But God has shown me that walking away from technology would mean walking away from gifts that He had given me to bring covenantal blessings into my life. Wisdom isn't about rejecting new things because they seem unfamiliar or daunting; it's about seeking understanding and discerning what comes from God and what is a distraction from the enemy.

## The Battle Between God's Gifts and the Enemy's Deceptions

We have to be very clear here: Technology is a tool, and like any tool, it can be used for good or for evil. Just as the Industrial Revolution brought incredible progress but also opened doors for exploitation, today's digital revolution presents us with a similar challenge. We are at a crossroads. On one side, God has given us technology—computers, the internet, AI, and more—as tools that can spread the gospel, foster connections, and bring prosperity. On the other side, the enemy tries to twist those very tools into instruments of distraction, fear, and destruction.

Ephesians 6:12 tells us, "For our struggle is not against flesh and blood, but against the rulers, against the authorities, against the powers of this dark world and against the spiritual forces of evil in the heavenly realms." This spiritual battle manifests in every part of our lives, and that includes the digital realm. The enemy wants to paralyze us with fear—fear of change, fear of technology, fear of the unknown. But God calls us to walk in wisdom, not fear.

## The Key Is Wisdom, Not Fear

I've realized that if I give in to fear—if I refuse to engage with technology because it feels overwhelming or the reality, I might just be afraid that I will not understand it or I will mess something up. I'm not just avoiding a new learning curve; I'm actively walking away from the blessings that God has prepared for me. God doesn't call us to cower in the face of change, but to face it with wisdom. James 1:5 says, *"If any of you lacks wisdom, you should ask God, who gives generously to all without finding fault, and it will be given to you."*

## GoSaferNet: A God-Given Vision

SaferNet wasn't just a business idea—it was a vision from God. I saw the immense value that today's technology could bring, but I also saw the dangers. The enemy wants to use the internet, apps, and AI to deceive, distract, and destroy. But God gave us the tools to stand firm, to protect ourselves and our families, and to use these technologies for His glory. He gave us the vision for a simple yet powerful cybersecurity tool that would allow people to access the internet safely—without the enemy's interference.

Just as Nehemiah rebuilt the walls of Jerusalem to protect God's people, we are building digital walls through SaferNet. Nehemiah 4:14 says, *"Don't be afraid of them. Remember the Lord, who is great and awesome, and fight for your families, your sons and your daughters, your wives and your homes."* We are not called to fear the enemy's attacks—we are called to fight, both spiritually and physically, for the things that God has entrusted to us.

## Advancing God's Plan Through Technology

Imagine how different the world could be if we all used technology as a tool to advance God's kingdom, free from the enemy's interference. Imagine a world where ministries could operate securely, families could connect safely, and businesses would thrive without the fear of cyberattacks. This is our vision for SaferNet. God gave us this tool, not just to protect people from hackers, but to enable them to live out their purpose, glorify God, and walk in His blessings—free from the enemy's distractions and destruction.

Psalm 127:1 says, *"Unless the Lord builds the house, the builders labor in vain."* We didn't create SaferNet on our own; we built it in partnership with God. And because of that, we know that this tool has the power to change lives—not just by securing data, but by enabling people to step into the fullness of God's plan for their lives.

## Walking in God's Wisdom in the Digital Age

At the end of the day, technology is here to stay. The question is not whether we should use it, but how we will use it. Will we allow fear to stop us from embracing the gifts that God has given us? Or will we step forward in wisdom, using these tools for His glory?

By walking in wisdom, educating ourselves about both the opportunities and the dangers, and partnering with God in every step, we can overcome the enemy's schemes and walk into the abundance that God has promised us. SaferNet is just one tool in this journey, but it's a tool that God has given us to protect His people and to advance His kingdom in this digital age.

# Chapter 14

## A Comprehensive Solution for Cybersecurity in a Digital World

Today's digital world faces increasing cyber threats. These threats are becoming more sophisticated and frequent. We need strong cybersecurity measures to protect ourselves. As Christians, we are called to be wise stewards of the resources and blessings that God has entrusted to us, including our personal data, communications, and the businesses that support our communities. SaferNet, a powerful cybersecurity tool, offers a comprehensive solution for protecting God's people online. With its 256-bit encrypted VPN, integrated virus protection, and over 200 internet controls, SaferNet is uniquely designed to safeguard everything from home networks to small and medium-sized businesses.

In this chapter, we will explore the technological capabilities of SaferNet, delve into the importance of its various cybersecurity features, and demonstrate how it can keep individuals and businesses safe from cybercrime, all while aligning with God's calling to protect what He has entrusted to us. But before we do this, I would like to tell you a little more about me and where my passion for cyber security comes from.

### The 256-Bit Encrypted VPN: A Fortress of Protection

At the heart of SaferNet's cybersecurity platform is its **256-bit encrypted VPN**. VPN stands for **Virtual Private Network**, a tool that allows users to create a secure, encrypted connection over the internet.

This encrypted "tunnel" protects the data traveling between your device and the websites or services you are accessing, making it virtually impossible for hackers to intercept or steal your information. Think of SaferNet's VPN as a secure path for your internet traffic. Just as you wouldn't send valuable mail without an envelope, you shouldn't send data without protection. SaferNet's VPN wraps your data in military-grade encryption.

The **256-bit encryption** used by SaferNet is one of the highest levels of encryption available today, commonly employed by industries such as banking, healthcare, and government institutions that handle highly sensitive data. This encryption level ensures that even if a hacker were to somehow intercept the data, it would be encrypted so thoroughly that it would be practically impossible to decrypt without the proper key. For context, breaking 256-bit encryption would take more time and computational power than is currently feasible, even with the most advanced supercomputers.

God's Word teaches us the importance of protecting our resources and guarding against theft and destruction. In Proverbs 4:23, we are told, "Above all else, guard your heart, for everything you do flows from it." Just as we are to guard our spiritual lives, we must also guard the digital data that represents our personal and professional identities. SaferNet's 256-bit encrypted VPN ensures that this vital task is accomplished by shielding users from prying eyes, whether they are accessing the internet from a secure home network or a public Wi-Fi connection.

## 24/7 Always-On VPN: Continuous Protection

One of SaferNet's most powerful features is its **24/7 always-on VPN**. This means that once the VPN is activated on a device, it remains active continuously, ensuring that every piece of data transmitted is protected by encryption. This is critical because, without a VPN, a user's internet traffic is exposed, and personal data like passwords, financial information, or even browsing habits can be intercepted by malicious actors.

The importance of an always-on VPN cannot be overstated. Cyberattacks can happen at any time, whether we are aware of them or not. By keeping the VPN constantly running, SaferNet guarantees that users are always protected, even if they forget to manually activate the VPN. This is particularly valuable when using public Wi-Fi networks, which are often unsecured and prime targets for hackers looking to steal data.

Just as Psalm 121:7 promises, "The Lord will keep you from all harm—He will watch over your life," SaferNet's always-on VPN acts as a vigilant guardian over your digital activities, ensuring that protection is in place even when you're not thinking about it. Now that we understand how VPNs protect us, let's look at how virus protection adds another layer of security.

## Virus Protection Built Into the VPN: Shielding Against Hidden Threats

Another cornerstone of SaferNet's security suite is its **built-in virus protection**, which works seamlessly alongside the VPN to prevent malware and other malicious programs from infecting devices. One of the most common ways viruses infiltrate a system is through visits to compromised or malicious websites. Even the most careful users can fall victim to these threats without realizing it, as cybercriminals often disguise malware within seemingly legitimate downloads or web pages.

SaferNet takes a proactive approach by scanning for and blocking access to websites known to harbor viruses, ransomware, or spyware. By integrating virus protection directly into the VPN, SaferNet ensures that users are not only safe from external data interception but also from dangerous content lurking on the internet. This integrated protection is particularly valuable because it operates quietly in the background, scanning for threats without disrupting the user's browsing experience.

The Bible speaks of being aware of the enemy's schemes. In 1 Peter 5:8, we are warned, "Be alert and of sober mind. Your enemy the devil prowls around like a roaring lion looking for someone to devour." Just as we must be vigilant against spiritual attacks, SaferNet ensures that we are vigilant against digital threats by preventing viruses from ever reaching our devices.

## Endpoint Device Protection: Securing Every Access Point

An **endpoint device** is any device that connects to a network or the internet. This includes computers, smartphones, tablets, and even IoT devices like smart thermostats or home security cameras. Every endpoint device represents a potential vulnerability in a network, as hackers can exploit unsecured devices to gain access to the larger network and its resources.

SaferNet provides protection for every endpoint device within its network. This means that once SaferNet is installed as an app on a device, it creates an encrypted VPN connection and begins actively defending against viruses, malware, and unauthorized access. By protecting each endpoint, SaferNet ensures that no single device can become the entry point for a cyberattack that could compromise the entire network.

This is especially important for businesses or households with multiple devices connected to the same network. If one device becomes infected with malware, it can spread to other devices on the network, causing widespread damage. SaferNet prevents this from happening by isolating each device with its own encrypted VPN tunnel, ensuring that even if one device encounters a threat, it cannot spread to others.

# Protection Against Ransomware: Rendering Cyberattacks Worthless

One of the most devastating types of cyberattacks today is **ransomware**. Ransomware is a form of malware that encrypts a user's files or entire system, making them inaccessible until the victim pays a ransom to the attacker. Ransomware attacks have crippled businesses, hospitals, and even entire city governments, often costing victims millions of dollars in ransom payments and downtime.

However, SaferNet's combination of virus protection and VPN security effectively neutralizes the threat of ransomware. By blocking malicious websites and preventing viruses from ever reaching a device, SaferNet eliminates the primary delivery method for ransomware. Even if a user were to accidentally open a harmful email or download a malicious file, SaferNet's virus protection would detect and contain the threat before it could spread to other devices on the network.

SaferNet provides important protection against many cyber threats. However, it's crucial to understand that no single security solution can prevent all types of attacks. For example, if a user downloads and opens a malicious file containing macro viruses, the damage may already be done before any security system can respond for that computer. The good news is that SaferNet will not allow that virus to transport itself to the network but that computer might be vulnerable. This is why we need multiple layers of protection, including:

- Safe email practices
- Regular software updates
- File scanning before opening
- Network protection through SaferNet
- Regular backups of important data

In this way, SaferNet renders ransomware attacks nearly worthless, as the malware never gets the chance to encrypt files or hold the system hostage. The Bible reminds us that God protects His people from harm. Isaiah 54:17 states, "No weapon forged against you will prevail." SaferNet serves as a digital shield, ensuring that the "weapons" of ransomware and other malware fail to infiltrate our devices and networks.

## Internet Controls and Filters: Tailoring Online Experiences

SaferNet offers over **200 internet controls**, including **84 content filters**, that allow users to customize and manage their online experiences. These filters cover a wide range of categories, from **adult content** and **violence** to **gambling**, **social media**, and even **proxy avoidance**. This feature is particularly valuable for parents, schools, and businesses that want to control what types of content are accessible on their networks.

For example, a family might use SaferNet's filters to block access to adult content, gambling sites, or any other inappropriate material. Similarly, a business might restrict access to social media or video streaming sites to ensure that employees remain productive. The filters can be fine-tuned to meet specific needs, allowing users to block or allow individual websites and applications as necessary.

SaferNet's internet controls provide an added layer of security by blocking websites known to distribute malware or engage in phishing scams. This reduces the risk of accidentally exposing devices or personal information to cybercriminals.

The Bible teaches us to guard our hearts and minds, and this principle extends to our digital lives. Philippians 4:8 urges us to think about things that are "true, noble, right, pure, lovely, admirable—if anything is excellent or praiseworthy." SaferNet's internet controls allow users to create an online environment that aligns with these values, blocking harmful content and keeping the focus on what is good and pure.

# Internet Time Management: Redeeming Time for God's Kingdom

One of the enemy's most subtle yet effective strategies is to waste our time, distracting us with endless scrolling, mindless entertainment, and activities that pull us away from fulfilling God's purpose in our lives. Ephesians 5:15-16 exhorts us to "be very careful, then, how you live—not as unwise but as wise, making the most of every opportunity because the days are evil." In the digital age, managing how we spend time online is crucial to staying focused on God's calling. SaferNet offers a powerful solution for this by allowing administrators to set time limits on any device connected to the internet, ensuring that users—whether children, employees, or even ourselves—spend the appropriate amount of time online. This feature is a safeguard against overconsumption of digital content and helps reclaim precious hours that can be devoted to prayer, study, work, and service in God's kingdom. With SaferNet, we can ensure that our time is spent wisely and purposefully, aligned with the divine calling to steward our lives effectively.

# Cloud-Based Admin Control: Managing Security from Anywhere

SaferNet's **cloud-based admin control** system allows administrators to manage all connected devices and internet controls from a single, centralized dashboard. This feature is ideal for families, small businesses, or organizations that need to monitor and control multiple devices across various locations. The admin can add or remove devices, adjust internet controls, and monitor all online activity from anywhere in the world.

This type of centralized control is typically only available to large corporations with dedicated IT teams and significant cybersecurity budgets. However, SaferNet provides this level of protection and oversight to individuals and small to medium-sized businesses at a fraction of the cost.

The admin control system is particularly valuable for businesses, where cybersecurity breaches can result in significant financial losses, legal liabilities, and damage to reputation. By giving business owners and IT managers the ability to monitor and control network activity in real time, SaferNet ensures that any suspicious activity is detected and addressed immediately.

## Why SaferNet Is Critical in Today's World

In a world where cybercrime is on the rise, SaferNet offers invaluable protection. With its 256-bit encrypted VPN, virus protection, internet controls, and cloud-based admin control, SaferNet is designed to keep individuals, families, and businesses safe from the wide array of online threats. Whether it's preventing identity theft, blocking ransomware attacks, or ensuring that employees stay productive, SaferNet provides the tools necessary to create a secure and efficient digital environment.

God calls us to be good stewards of the resources He has given us, and that includes our personal data, our businesses, and our families. SaferNet allows us to fulfill this responsibility by offering a comprehensive solution that protects against the dangers of the digital world. Proverbs 27:12 says, "The prudent see danger and take refuge, but the simple keep going and pay the penalty." SaferNet gives us the ability to take refuge from the dangers of cybercrime, providing the peace of mind that comes from knowing we are protected.

## SaferNet as a Guardian of God's People Online

SaferNet is not just a piece of software; it is a guardian in the digital world, keeping God's people safe from the myriad of online dangers. From protecting endpoint devices with 256-bit encryption to blocking malware and ransomware, SaferNet provides comprehensive security that is both practical and aligned with God's calling for us to protect what has been entrusted to our care.

In a world where cyber threats are increasingly sophisticated, SaferNet stands as a powerful tool that individuals, families, and businesses can use to ensure their safety and productivity. By leveraging its advanced features, we can create a secure digital environment that allows us to focus on what truly matters—living out our faith, stewarding our resources, and contributing to the communities around us.

Although SaferNet is a robust and powerful cybersecurity solution, there is no single tool that can guarantee complete protection for families or small to medium-sized businesses (SMBs) in every scenario. Cyber threats evolve rapidly, and while SaferNet continuously adapts to address emerging risks, a multi-layered system is critical for comprehensive security in today's digital landscape. By combining SaferNet's encrypted VPN, virus protection, and internet controls with additional measures such as strong password management, multi-factor authentication, regular software updates, and employee training on phishing awareness, users can build a more resilient defense against the ever-changing array of cyber threats. This multi-system approach ensures that vulnerabilities are minimized, providing enhanced safety in a world where digital risks are constantly evolving.

## Additional Cyber Security Protocols Beyond SaferNet: A Comprehensive Approach for Families and Small to Medium-Sized Businesses

While **SaferNet** provides a robust cybersecurity solution with its 256-bit encrypted VPN, virus protection, 200 internet controls, and cloud-based admin capabilities, achieving comprehensive cybersecurity requires a multi-layered approach. For families and small to medium-sized businesses (SMBs), implementing additional protocols will strengthen the overall security posture and mitigate other risks that SaferNet alone may not fully address. Cybercriminals are constantly evolving their tactics, and businesses and individuals must be prepared with proactive defenses.

Here are several additional cybersecurity protocols that families and SMBs should adopt in conjunction with SaferNet to ensure full protection:

## Regular Software and Firmware Updates

Keeping all software and firmware up to date is a critical but often overlooked aspect of cybersecurity. Cybercriminals frequently exploit vulnerabilities in outdated software to gain unauthorized access to systems. Regular updates to your operating system (e.g., Windows, macOS, iOS) and software applications ensure that these vulnerabilities are patched. Furthermore, devices like routers, IoT gadgets, and networked printers require **firmware updates** to close security loopholes. Many IoT devices, in particular, have limited security features, making them prime targets for cyberattacks. Setting your devices to automatically install updates ensures you stay protected, reducing the risk of being exploited through unpatched software.

## Regular Data Backups

While SaferNet protects your devices and networks from malware and ransomware attacks, implementing regular data backup protocols is essential for recovering critical files in case of a cyberattack, hardware failure, or accidental deletion. Ransomware can encrypt your files, rendering them inaccessible unless a ransom is paid. However, if you have recent backups, you can restore your data without complying with the attackers' demands. Using **cloud backup** services like **Google Drive**, **Dropbox**, or **Backblaze** allows you to store copies of your files offsite, safeguarding them from local cyberattacks or hardware failures. Additionally, maintaining an **offline backup** on an external hard drive provides further protection by keeping a copy of your data completely disconnected from the network.

# Network Segmentation

**Network segmentation** is the practice of dividing a network into smaller, isolated segments to limit the spread of a cyberattack. If one segment is compromised, the breach will not affect the entire network. This is especially useful for families or small to medium-sized businesses (SMBs) that have a variety of devices with different security needs. For instance, a child's tablet or smart TV may not require the same level of access as a business's accounting system. Many routers offer the ability to create **guest networks** that restrict access to internal resources, while SMBs can segment critical business systems from general office or guest access.

# Virus Protection for Your Computer

While SaferNet offers advanced malware protection through its always-on VPN and 24/7 internet security features, no single tool can provide complete virus protection. SaferNet is incredibly effective as long as it remains connected, but there may be instances when the VPN is disconnected—whether intentionally or due to technical issues. In such cases, having a backup antivirus or anti-malware solution installed on your computer is crucial. Most computers come with built-in or free antivirus software, like Windows Defender, which serves as an excellent secondary layer of defense. This backup ensures that, even when SaferNet is offline, your device is still protected from malware, viruses, and other cyber threats. Utilizing both SaferNet and a backup antivirus provides a dual layer of security, minimizing vulnerabilities and enhancing your overall protection.

# Email Phishing Awareness and Security Training

Email phishing is one of the most effective ways for hackers to gain access to a system. Phishing emails often contain malicious attachments or links that can infect devices or steal login credentials. Conducting **phishing simulations** and providing **security training** for employees or family members is essential for building awareness

200

and reducing the risk of phishing attacks. **Advanced email filtering** tools, such as **Barracuda** or **Proofpoint**, can block phishing attempts before they reach your inbox. Educating users about the common signs of phishing emails—such as urgent requests, unfamiliar links, and suspicious attachments—can further minimize risks.

## Firewall Protection

While SaferNet offers excellent protection through its VPN and internet controls, implementing a **firewall** is an additional security measure that helps control the flow of traffic between your network and external networks. A firewall acts as a barrier that filters incoming and outgoing traffic based on predefined security rules. It blocks unauthorized access while allowing legitimate traffic to pass through. This is especially important for SMBs, as firewalls prevent hackers from accessing sensitive business data by blocking suspicious activity at the network level. A **hardware firewall** (such as those built into routers) or a **software firewall** (like Windows Firewall) adds an extra layer of security to your network.

## Physical Security of Devices

Even with robust digital security like SaferNet in place, physical access to devices can still pose a risk. If a device is stolen or misplaced, unauthorized individuals could access sensitive data or compromise the system. Securing devices with **laptop locks** or keeping them in physical safes when not in use adds a layer of protection against theft. Setting devices to **automatically lock** after a short period of inactivity and requiring biometric authentication, such as fingerprints or facial recognition, ensures that unauthorized users cannot easily access your devices.

## A Multi-Layered Approach to Cybersecurity

SaferNet provides a powerful and comprehensive solution that addresses many critical aspects of cybersecurity, including VPN protection, malware prevention, and internet controls. However, no single tool can cover all potential risks, and a **multi-layered approach** is essential for ensuring complete security. By combining SaferNet with additional cybersecurity protocols such as strong password management, regular software updates, data backups, network segmentation, email phishing awareness, firewall protection, and physical device security, individuals and SMBs can build a more resilient defense against the growing array of cyber threats. As stewards of God's resources, it is our responsibility to protect not only our financial and physical assets but also the digital assets that are becoming an increasingly important part of our everyday lives.

## Basic Cyber Security Protocol for Those Not Using SaferNet

While SaferNet offers a comprehensive, multi-tool approach to foundational cybersecurity, we understand that not everyone will choose to use it as their primary security solution. For those opting to manage their own cybersecurity without the integrated tools of SaferNet, it's essential to follow a detailed protocol that incorporates multiple layers of protection to defend against the ever-present threats in today's digital world. Below is a basic yet robust cybersecurity protocol designed for families, individuals, and small to medium-sized businesses (SMBs) that choose to operate without SaferNet.

## Comprehensive Cybersecurity Without SaferNet: A Detailed Technical Approach

If SaferNet is not being used, achieving robust cybersecurity requires the implementation of a multi-layered approach involving several advanced tools and protocols. In this guide, we will explore the necessary components to protect systems, networks, and users from a variety of cyber threats. Each element—firewalls, antivirus software, encryption, multi-factor authentication, network monitoring, and more—serves a critical role in forming a cohesive defense strategy.

This highly technical approach requires attention to detail and continuous maintenance to stay effective.

## Firewall Protection: Network Traffic Control and Threat Prevention

A **firewall** is one of the most fundamental components of any cybersecurity strategy. It acts as a barrier between your internal network and external networks (like the internet) and controls the flow of traffic based on predefined rules. Without SaferNet's integrated protections, a **Next-Generation Firewall (NGFW)** becomes crucial.

**Types of Firewalls**: **Packet Filtering Firewalls** examine data packets based on source and destination IP addresses, port numbers, and protocols. These are simple but inadequate for handling advanced attacks. **Stateful Inspection Firewalls** monitor the state of active connections, offering more comprehensive protection by evaluating the context of each data packet. **Next-Generation Firewalls (NGFWs)** include deep packet inspection and advanced threat detection capabilities, such as intrusion prevention and malware scanning. NGFWs are critical for detecting and preventing sophisticated cyberattacks, such as zero-day exploits. Firewalls serve as the first line of defense in regulating data traffic. **Hardware firewalls** like Cisco Firepower or **software firewalls** like pfSense or Sophos are highly recommended for securing complex networks. By controlling traffic flow and preventing unauthorized access, they offer a strong security perimeter, which is especially important in business environments.

## Endpoint Protection: Comprehensive Antivirus and Malware Defense

Endpoint protection is essential in securing every device that connects to your network. Without SaferNet's always-on malware protection, deploying a **robust Endpoint Protection Platform (EPP)** combined with **Endpoint Detection and Response (EDR)** is necessary to safeguard devices from malware, ransomware, and advanced persistent threats.

**Key Elements**: **Signature-based detection** relies on known malware signatures but is insufficient for detecting newer, more sophisticated threats. **Heuristic and Behavioral Analysis** monitors the behavior of programs to detect malicious activity, even if the threat is previously unknown or polymorphic. **Ransomware Protection** prevents ransomware from encrypting files by using techniques like file integrity monitoring and automatic rollback of compromised files. **Sandboxing** isolates potentially malicious files, allowing them to be executed and observed in a secure environment before they are allowed to run on the main system.

Tools like **Symantec Endpoint Protection, CrowdStrike Falcon**, or **Bitdefender GravityZone** offer advanced features such as real-time monitoring, deep scanning, and advanced threat detection. Endpoint protection is particularly important for preventing data breaches from phishing attacks or compromised downloads.

# Data Encryption: Securing Data at Rest and In Transit

Without SaferNet's 256-bit encrypted VPN, securing data with encryption technologies is vital to protect against interception during transmission and ensure the confidentiality of stored data.

**Data Encryption Technologies**: **Transport Layer Security (TLS)** provides encryption for data in transit over networks, ensuring secure communication between client devices and servers. **Full Disk Encryption (FDE)**, such as **BitLocker** (Windows) or **FileVault** (macOS), encrypts entire storage drives, safeguarding data even if the device is physically stolen. **End-to-End Encryption (E2EE)** ensures that only the sender and recipient can decrypt messages or data, preventing third-party access even if the communication is intercepted.

Encryption prevents sensitive information like financial data, intellectual property, or personal information from being exposed. By ensuring all communications and stored data are encrypted, businesses and individuals can protect against data theft and unauthorized access, especially in high-risk environments.

## Multi-Factor Authentication (MFA) and Identity Access Management (IAM)

In the absence of SaferNet's VPN, robust **Multi-Factor Authentication (MFA)** and **Identity and Access Management (IAM)** solutions are critical to protecting user accounts from unauthorized access due to compromised passwords.

**Components of MFA and IAM**: **MFA** adds a second layer of authentication, typically combining something the user knows (password), something they have (mobile device or token), and something they are (biometrics). **IAM** solutions ensure that users have the correct permissions for accessing specific resources, adhering to the principle of **least privilege**, which limits user access to only what is necessary.

MFA reduces the risk of unauthorized access, even if passwords are compromised. IAM systems centralize user access management and ensure that permissions are appropriate for each user's role. Implementing **Okta**, **Duo Security**, or **Microsoft Azure Active Directory** provides a strong defense against compromised login credentials.

## Network Segmentation and Intrusion Detection Systems (IDS/IPS)

**Network segmentation** and **Intrusion Detection Systems (IDS)** or **Intrusion Prevention Systems (IPS)** are crucial for limiting the scope of an attack and identifying malicious activity early.

**Network Segmentation**: Dividing the network into isolated segments prevents an attacker from moving laterally across systems. For example, separating critical business systems (like accounting) from general employee networks reduces the impact of a breach. Setting up **guest networks** for visitors or IoT devices minimizes the risk that these lower-security devices could expose the broader network to attack.

**IDS/IPS**: **IDS** monitors network traffic for signs of malicious activity, alerting administrators to potential threats. **IPS** actively blocks suspicious traffic and takes preventive action against intrusions.

By implementing solutions like **Cisco Stealthwatch** or **Snort (IDS)**, organizations can detect and respond to attacks in real-time, significantly reducing the damage caused by cyber threats. **IPS** tools, such as **Palo Alto Networks**, combine intrusion prevention with advanced firewalls to ensure that threats are detected and blocked before they can cause harm.

## Regular Software and Firmware Updates

Keeping software and firmware up to date is an essential but often neglected aspect of cybersecurity. **Unpatched vulnerabilities** in outdated software are a frequent target for attackers looking to exploit weaknesses in systems.

**Key Actions**: Regularly update all **operating systems**, web browsers, and third-party applications to ensure they are patched against the latest vulnerabilities. Ensure that **firmware updates** for routers, IoT devices, and networked printers are regularly applied to close security loopholes.

Many systems allow for **automatic updates**, which reduces the risk of human error and ensures that all systems remain secure. Tools like **SolarWinds Patch Manager** automate the patch management process for businesses, ensuring that no vulnerabilities remain unpatched.

# Data Backups: Mitigating the Risk of Ransomware

Without SaferNet's built-in protection against ransomware, regular and reliable **data backups** become a critical safeguard. Ransomware can lock users out of their systems by encrypting files and demanding payment for decryption keys.

**Backup Solutions**: **Cloud Backups** ensure that data is securely stored offsite, providing protection against both local attacks and hardware failures. **Local Offline Backups** on external hard drives add another layer of protection. These should be stored offline to prevent ransomware from reaching them.

**Google Drive**, **Dropbox**, or **Backblaze** are popular cloud backup services, while external hard drives provide additional offline backup options. Regular backups ensure that even if ransomware strikes, data can be recovered without having to pay a ransom.

# Email Phishing Awareness and Security Training

Phishing remains one of the most common methods attackers use to gain access to systems. Employees and users need to be trained to recognize phishing attempts and suspicious emails.

**Training and Simulations**: Conduct **phishing simulations** to help users recognize fake emails and malicious links. Implement **advanced email filtering** tools like **Barracuda** or **Proofpoint**, which scan incoming emails for phishing attempts and malware.

Regular phishing awareness training builds a culture of vigilance, reducing the likelihood of successful attacks via compromised emails.

# Security Information and Event Management (SIEM)

For organizations with complex infrastructure, a **Security Information and Event Management (SIEM)** system is essential for real-time monitoring and incident response.

**SIEM Capabilities**: SIEM systems aggregate logs from all network devices, including firewalls, servers, and endpoint devices, providing a comprehensive overview of security events. Advanced threat detection algorithms in SIEM solutions identify anomalies or suspicious activity, alerting administrators to potential breaches.

Implementing tools like **Splunk** or **IBM QRadar** enables businesses to detect threats early, respond effectively, and ensure compliance with regulations like **GDPR** or **HIPAA**.

# Implementing a Multi-Layered Cybersecurity Defense Without SaferNet

While SaferNet provides a simplified and integrated solution for securing devices, networks, and data, achieving comprehensive cybersecurity without it requires the implementation of multiple advanced technologies and protocols. From firewalls and endpoint protection to encryption and SIEM, each element plays a critical role in defending against the ever-growing threat landscape. These solutions, while highly effective, require ongoing management, technical expertise, and proactive monitoring to ensure that vulnerabilities are minimized, and assets remain secure. By employing a multi-layered defense, businesses and individuals can achieve a level of security that is robust enough to combat the wide range of cyber threats present in today's digital world.

**As we conclude this section on** *"Unshakable Digital Defense: God's Blueprint for Physical and Spiritual Protection in a Technological World,"* it's clear that God's desire is for His people to live protected, abundant lives, both spiritually and physically. In today's digital age, cybersecurity is no longer just a technical issue—it's a spiritual one, too. Just as we put on the Armor of God to guard against spiritual attacks, we must also equip ourselves with the practical tools necessary to defend against cyber threats.

The digital world offers immense opportunities for spreading God's word, growing businesses, and connecting with others, but it also presents new risks. By taking proactive steps like using firewalls, VPNs, and multi-factor authentication, and of course SaferNet we can shield ourselves from the enemy's schemes, ensuring that our data, identities, and ministries remain secure.

Consider the story of Nehemiah, who, with faith and determination, rebuilt the walls of Jerusalem to protect his people from outside threats. Today, we are called to build strong digital walls—safeguards that ensure our online spaces are protected from harm. Just as Nehemiah trusted in God's provision and guidance, we can trust that God has equipped us with the wisdom and tools necessary to thrive in this new digital era.

This is your call to action: partner with God in securing not only your spiritual life but also your digital one. Start by implementing the cybersecurity measures discussed in this section, knowing that every step you take fortifies your digital life in alignment with God's protective hand. Together, let us continue building a world where technology is used for God's glory, free from the enemy's interference. With faith, vigilance, and the right tools, we can embrace the digital age while standing strong in God's eternal promises.

As we wrap up this section on *"Unshakable Digital Defense: God's Blueprint for Physical and Spiritual Protection in a Technological World,"* one of the most important steps you can take today is to go to SaferNetVPN.com and sign up for SaferNet. By doing so, you will be starting one of the easiest and simplest ways to keep yourself safe online.

Just as we put on the Armor of God daily, taking this small but essential step will ensure you are shielded from the digital threats that surround us. SaferNet offers robust protection—encrypting your internet, guarding against malware, and ensuring your online activity remains secure. It's an effortless yet powerful way to protect your personal data, your family, and your business, allowing you to confidently use technology as a tool for God's glory.

By signing up for SaferNet, you are taking control of your digital safety while partnering with God to safeguard what He has entrusted to you. Now is the time to act—secure your online world with the protection and wisdom God has provided.

As we conclude our exploration of digital security, remember that protecting yourself online is a vital part of modern stewardship. Just as we put on the Armor of God daily, we must also implement strong digital protection. This can take many forms:

- Using a trusted VPN service to encrypt your internet traffic
- Installing reliable antivirus software
- Implementing content filters to protect your family
- Setting up time management tools to maintain healthy online boundaries
- Utilizing cloud-based security solutions

SaferNet offers these protections in one integrated package, making it easier to implement comprehensive security. However, regardless of which tools you choose, the important thing is to take action to protect what God has entrusted to you.

Remember Nehemiah's example - he didn't just pray for protection; he took practical steps to build strong walls. Similarly, we must combine our faith with action in the digital world. Whether through SaferNet or other security measures, establishing strong digital protection allows you to use technology confidently as a tool for God's glory while guarding against modern threats.

Take time to evaluate your current digital security and consider what steps you need to take. The tools are available - now it's up to you to implement them wisely and prayerfully

# Chapter 15

## Conclusion: The Call to Rise – A Digital Battle Worth Fighting

L et me leave you with a story, one that encapsulates everything we've journeyed through together, everything you've fought to understand, and everything you'll need to face moving forward.

It was an ordinary day, or so it seemed. I was in the thick of the busyness we all experience—emails filling up the inbox, meetings lined up, and the constant hum of digital noise. But beneath the surface, something darker was unfolding. **I had been hacked**. But this was no ordinary cyberattack; this was an invasion. My business, my family, my life's work—all of it was under siege. And as I stared at the screen, watching it all unravel in front of me, **I felt the weight of more than just lost data**. This was a spiritual attack—**an assault from the enemy himself**.

The Bible tells us in **John 10:10** that "the thief comes only to steal, kill, and destroy," and that's exactly what I felt was happening. But I also remembered the second half of that verse: **"I have come that they may have life and have it abundantly."** This wasn't just about a cybersecurity breach; this was a battle for the abundant life God had promised me. It was a battle for my peace, my purpose, my calling. And I had a choice to make. I could crumble in fear, or I could rise and fight, not just in the physical but in the spiritual realm where this battle truly resided.

Making the choice to stand and fight changed everything. I discovered I wasn't alone. God had equipped me with both spiritual armor and practical tools. He had given me the wisdom to navigate this digital storm, just as **James 1:5** promises: "If any of you lacks wisdom, you should ask God, who gives generously to all without finding fault, and it will be given to you." God was with me in the fight, guiding me, arming me with knowledge, and reminding me that technology, when stewarded under His direction, is a **gift**, not a curse.

This is your story too.

## A Battle You Cannot Afford to Ignore

As you reach the end of this book, I need you to remember something critical: **this is not just a book about technology**. This is about the battle for your soul, your family, your business, and your relationship with God. The stakes have never been higher.

**Ephesians 6:12** reminds us that "our struggle is not against flesh and blood but against the rulers, against the authorities, against the powers of this dark world and against the spiritual forces of evil in the heavenly realms." Every day, you stand at the crossroads where the digital and the spiritual meet. The enemy knows this, and he is relentless in his pursuit to steal your joy, disrupt your peace, and divert you from God's purposes.

The tools he uses. Technology. The very devices we rely on to live, work, and communicate have become the enemy's playground. He uses social media to breed envy and division, the internet to spread lies and deception, and cyberattacks to sow fear and chaos. But here's the truth: **God is calling you to take a stand**. To be vigilant, both spiritually and practically, and to reclaim the digital world for His glory.

You are not just called to exist in this digital age; you are called to **thrive**. **Joshua 1:9** commands us: "Have I not commanded you? Be strong and courageous. Do not be afraid; do not be discouraged, for the Lord your God will be with you wherever you go." That includes the digital realm. God is calling you to fight for what He has entrusted to you—to protect your family, your work, and your faith from the enemy's schemes.

And now is the time to step into this new digital age **like never before**. **This is not a time to shrink back or be timid**. It is the time to **embrace technology with boldness**, to learn what you've never learned, and to use the tools that God has given you to their fullest capacity. This is your moment to create that **podcast that brings glory to God**, to build that **website that changes people's lives**, to **start that business** that God has laid on your heart, and to use the technology of this age to **advance His Kingdom** without fear and without hesitation.

## The Power of Saying Yes

Let me tell you about a friend of mine's wife. She, like many, was overwhelmed by technology. Every time she logged on to her computer, a flood of fear came over her—fear of being hacked, fear of falling for a scam, fear of the unknown. But instead of giving in to fear, **she made a choice**. She chose to step into the battle, to learn, to grow, and to protect her family from the very things that frightened her.

**Proverbs 31:25** speaks of the woman of noble character: "She is clothed with strength and dignity; she can laugh at the days to come." My friend stepped into her role as protector of her home and family, not by cowering in fear but by trusting God and using the wisdom He provided. She embraced the tools laid out in this book, learning to navigate the digital landscape with both confidence and caution. And the result? Not only did she protect her family, but she also found **new ways to serve God** online. One day, a stranger across the globe found her story—her testimony of faith in the face of fear—and that stranger came to know Christ.

**God can use your willingness to engage** in the digital world for His glory. What if my friend had refused to fight? What if she had allowed fear to keep her from stepping into her calling? That soul might still be lost. **What about you?**

Imagine the lives you could touch if you **boldly stepped into this digital age**. Imagine the impact of that podcast, that business, that message you've been holding back. **This is your time**—God has equipped you with the knowledge, wisdom, and courage you need to **create, innovate, and expand** His Kingdom like never before.

## A Call to Action: Step into the Fight

This is your moment. This is where you decide whether you will be a passive bystander in the digital age or **a warrior**. Will you allow the enemy to use technology to disrupt your life, or will you take a stand, using it for God's purposes?

**Romans 12:21** tells us, "Do not be overcome by evil, but overcome evil with good." You have the tools and the wisdom to do just that. You are not helpless in this fight. You have been given the **armor of God**, as described in **Ephesians 6**: the belt of truth, the breastplate of righteousness, the gospel of peace, the shield of faith, the helmet of salvation, and the sword of the Spirit. These aren't just spiritual concepts—they are practical strategies you can apply to protect your digital life.

There will be days when it feels overwhelming. Days when the digital noise is too loud, and the enemy's attacks feel too strong. But **you are not alone**. **Isaiah 41:10** promises, "So do not fear, for I am with you; do not be dismayed, for I am your God. I will strengthen you and help you; I will uphold you with my righteous right hand." God is with you in this fight, and He has already equipped you with everything you need to stand firm.

The battlefield has shifted, and the digital realm is where much of the fight is happening now. But God is calling you to **move forward**. Step into the **digital age** with confidence, **learn** what you've never learned before, and **create** what you've never dared to create. This is the time to be **bold**—to use technology as the **powerful tool** it is meant to be, a tool for **building His Kingdom**.

# The Final Word: The World is Waiting

So, what will you do? Will you shrink back in fear? Will you let the enemy steal your peace, your family's security, and your calling? Or will you rise up and say **yes** to the abundant life God has promised you?

**John 16:33** gives us this encouragement from Jesus: "In this world, you will have trouble. But take heart! I have overcome the world." This includes the digital world. You don't have to fear what technology might bring. **God has already overcome it**.

The world is waiting for you to lead. Your family needs you to protect them. Your business needs you to step into this new age with wisdom and courage. Your ministry needs your voice online, sharing God's truth in a space that desperately needs it. And most of all, **God is waiting for you to rise up and say yes**.

This is your call to action. The digital battlefield is real, but you are not powerless. You are equipped with both the spiritual and technological tools to **win this fight**. So, rise. Take hold of the wisdom, the strategy, and the strength that God has already given you. And never forget **you were made for such a time as this (Esther 4:14)**.

Now is your moment to rise up and **reclaim the digital world for God's glory**. You stand equipped with both spiritual and practical armor - the tools from this book, the strength of God's Spirit, and the unshakable truth of His Word. Remember **Esther 4:14 - you were made for such a time as this**. Whether through podcasts that bring hope, websites that share truth, or businesses that serve His kingdom, your gifts are needed in this digital age. Let the enemy's schemes fall powerless as you step forward in bold faith. The time for hesitation is over. The time for fear is past. **Now is the time to fight. Now is the time to win.** Now is the time to step into this digital age like never before, knowing that God goes before you in every step.

# Book Review: "God, the Devil, and the Internet"

*"God, the Devil, and the Internet"* offers a transformative exploration of the digital world, guiding readers to harness the immense power of technology while staying rooted in their faith. At its core, the book is about helping people understand the complexities of new technology so they can use the internet to reduce risk, enhance their lives, and bring them closer to the abundance God intends for them. Rather than viewing the internet as something to be feared, this book celebrates it as a tool God has gifted humanity—a tool designed for connection, prosperity, and blessing.

**Understanding the Purpose Behind the Internet**

The author presents a compelling case that the internet, like any other tool, was originally intended by God to bless His people. The book explains that while the enemy desires to use this same technology to distract, mislead, or destroy lives, believers can and should harness its power for good. By navigating the internet with wisdom, believers can experience greater purpose, prosperity, and protection in their personal and professional lives. The internet isn't something to shy away from—it's something to embrace with the right knowledge and spiritual discernment.

**Reducing Risks While Embracing Opportunities**

"God, the Devil, and the Internet" serves as a comprehensive guide to help readers mitigate the risks associated with online activity while maximizing the potential for success. Through practical steps, cybersecurity insights, and spiritual reflection, the book equips readers with the tools they need to stay safe and grounded in their faith. Readers will learn how to use firewalls, VPNs, and other modern

216

protections to ensure that they can confidently navigate the digital landscape without falling victim to online threats.

## Celebrating God's Gift of the Internet

At its heart, this book encourages believers to see the internet as a gift from God—an opportunity for connection, growth, and abundance. The internet, when used correctly, can be a powerful tool for building businesses, spreading the gospel, and nurturing relationships. This book teaches readers how to utilize technology to its fullest potential, aligning their online activities with God's purpose while safeguarding themselves from the enemy's tactics.

## For Small and Medium-Sized Businesses

The book also offers invaluable insights for small and medium-sized business owners, showing them how to leverage the internet for growth while minimizing cybersecurity risks. Business leaders will find practical advice on how to protect their digital assets and ensure that their online presence reflects their values and supports their mission. Whether it's through protecting customer data or using technology to create opportunities, this book is a guide for businesses seeking to thrive in the digital age.

## A Call to Embrace Technology for Good

*"God, the Devil, and the Internet"* empowers readers to embrace the digital world as part of God's plan, helping them stay focused on His blessings while safeguarding against the enemy's distractions. This book will inspire believers to see the internet not as a threat, but as a powerful tool that can be used to glorify God, build community, and create a life of abundance. Whether for personal use or business growth, readers will walk away with the confidence to navigate the online world safely and purposefully.